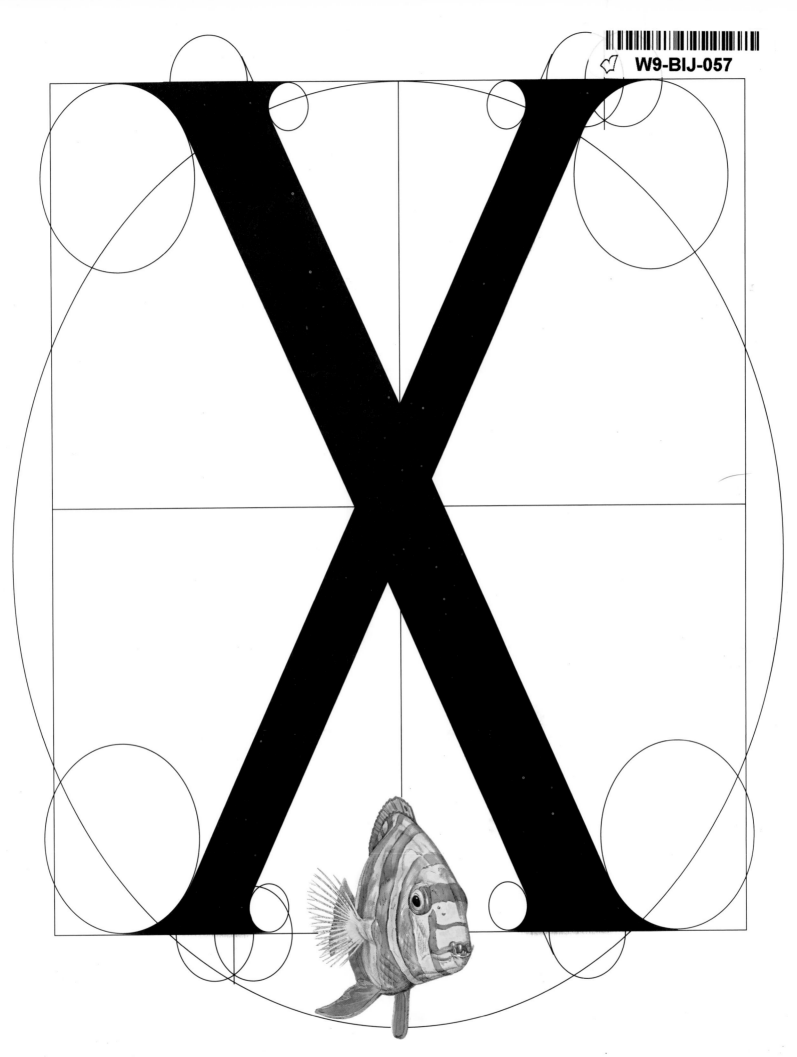

THE X-RAY PICTURE BOOK *of* AMAZING ANIMALS

Author:

Gerald Legg holds a doctorate in zoology from Manchester University. He has worked in West Africa for several years as lecturer and rain forest researcher. Dr Legg's current position is biologist at the Booth Museum of Natural History in Brighton; he is also continuing his research on rain forests.

Creator:

David Salariya was born in Dundee, Scotland, where he studied illustration and printmaking, concentrating on book design in his post-graduate year. He has illustrated a wide range of books on botanical, historical and mythical subjects. He has designed and created the *Timelines*, *New View* and *X-ray Picture Book* series for Watts. He lives in Brighton with his wife, the illustrator Shirley Willis.

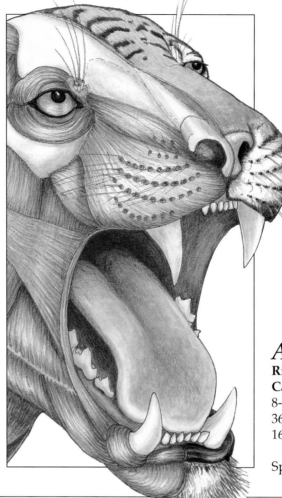

David Salariya *Series Editor*
Ruth Taylor *Senior Editor*
Kathryn Senior *Editor*
Steve Longdale *Assistant Design*

Artists:

Richard Coombes
Catherine Constable
Ryz Hajdul
Emily Mayer
Carolyn Scrace

Artists:

Richard Coombes 34-35,42-43, 44-45; **Catherine Constable** 22-23; **Ryz Hajdul** 6-7, 8-9; **Emily Mayer** 26-27, 28-29, 30-31, 32-33, 36-37; **Carolyn Scrace** 10-11, 12-13, 14-15, 16-17, 18-19, 20-21, 24-25, 38-39, 40-41.

Special thanks to Carolyn Scrace.

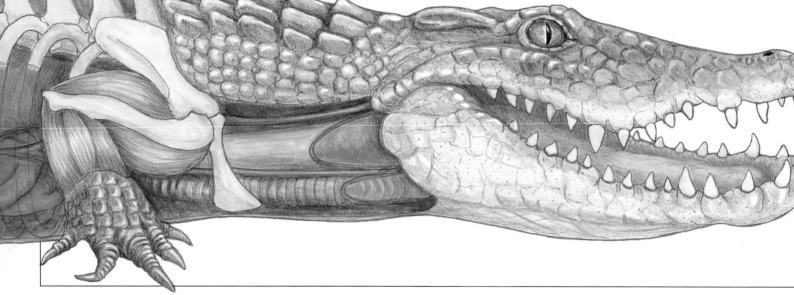

Franklin Watts
95 Madison Avenue
New York, NY 10016

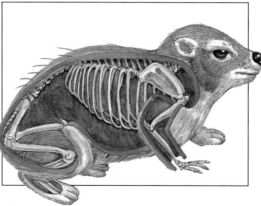

© The Salariya Book Co Ltd 1993

Library of Congress Cataloging-in-Publication Data
Legg, Gerald.
    Amazing animals / written by Gerald Legg;
    created and designed by David Salariya.
    p.   cm. (The X-ray picture book)
    Includes index.
    ISBN 0-531-14285-X (lib.bdg.) –
    ISBN 0-531-15708-3 (pbk.)
    1. Animals – Juvenile literature. 2. Anatomy,
Comparative – Juvenile literature. [1. Animals.
2. Anatomy, Comparative.]
I. Salariya, David. II. Title.
QL49.L373   1994
591.4–dc20
                                    93-36703
                                    CIP AC

The X RAY PICTURE BOOK of AMAZING ANIMALS

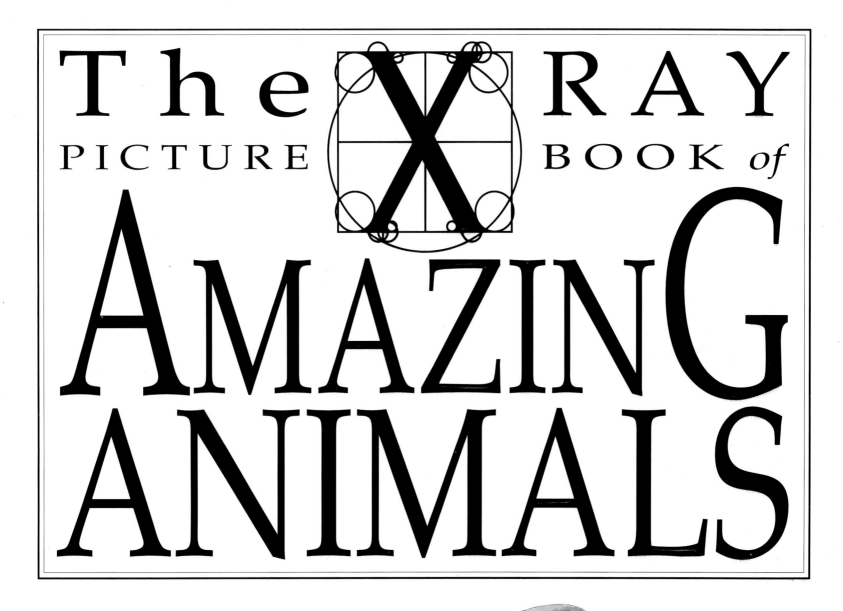

Written by
GERALD LEGG

Created and designed by
DAVID SALARIYA

FRANKLIN WATTS

NEW YORK • CHICAGO • LONDON • TORONTO • SYDNEY

CONTENTS

THE FLY

6

A TRÙE FLY is an insect with two wings. There are over 90,000 species of fly living in a variety of habitats. The common housefly has a life expectancy of three weeks.

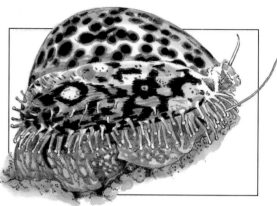

THE SNAIL

10

SNAILS belong to a strange group of animals called gastropods. Gastropod means "foot stomach." The shell of a snail is a complex structure which protects its body.

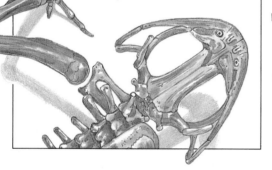

THE FROG

14

THE FROG is probably the most successful of all amphibians. Frogs' eggs hatch into tadpoles which gradually change into adults by gaining limbs and losing their tails.

THE FISH

18

FISH ARE VERTEBRATES - they have a backbone and an internal skeleton. They live in water, breathe through gills, have a scaly body and swim using fins.

THE SNAKE

22

THE SNAKE is a legless reptile with a long scaly-skinned body. It lays eggs from which live young hatch. Although without limbs, it is an effective hunter and killer.

THE BIRD

26

A BIRD is a warm-blooded animal with two legs, a beak and a pair of wings. Most are efficient flying machines. Birds are the only animals which have feathers.

THE RAT

30

RATS are warm-blooded mammals that suckle their young with milk produced by mammary glands. Fleas that live on rats can spread disease to people.

THE TIGER

34

TIGERS are carnivores, members of the big cat family. They are patient hunters, with razor-sharp teeth. Tigers eat most of their prey except for some bones and the hooves.

THE ELEPHANT

38

THE ELEPHANT is the largest living land mammal, measuring about 13 feet (4 m) high and weighing around 5,500 lbs (12,000 kg). It has huge ears, a strong trunk and large tusks.

THE WHALE

42

WHALES are huge sea mammals. The blue whale weighs around 30 tons (150,000 kg) and can live to be 45 years old. Despite their size, whales are gentle and graceful.

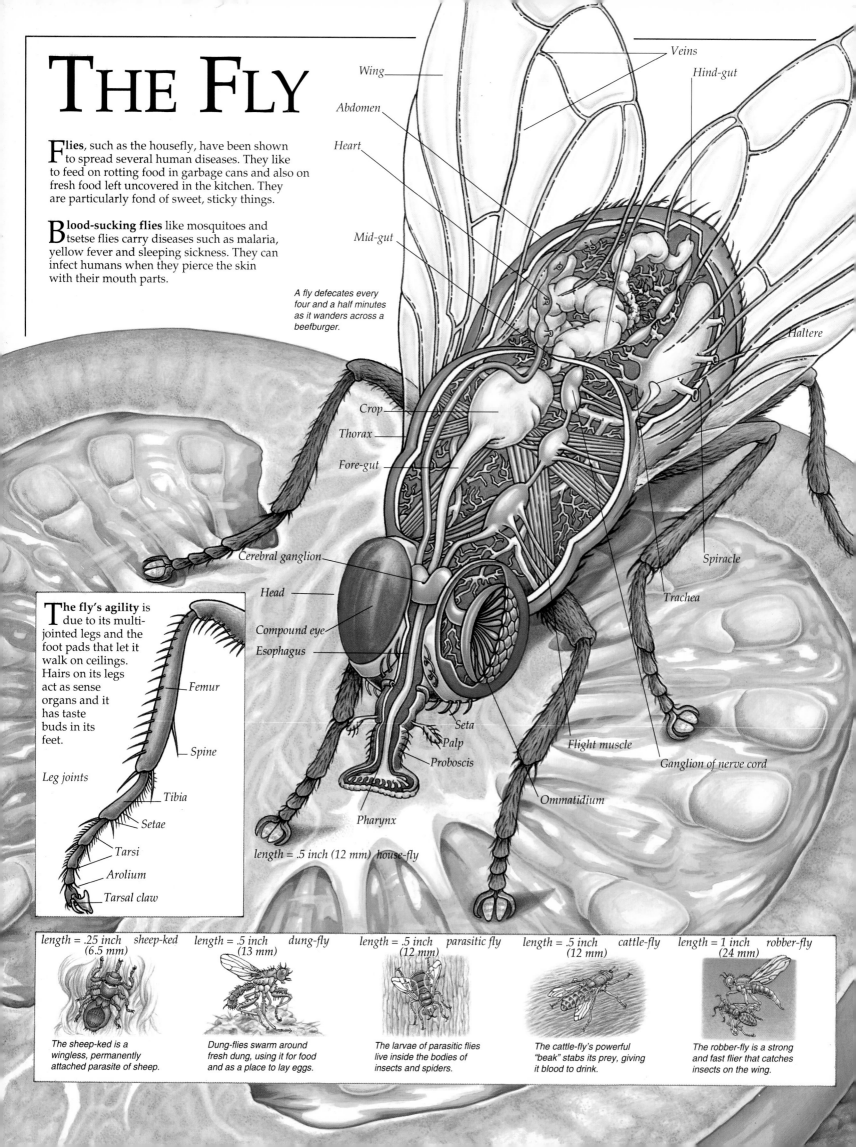

THE FLY

Flies, such as the housefly, have been shown to spread several human diseases. They like to feed on rotting food in garbage cans and also on fresh food left uncovered in the kitchen. They are particularly fond of sweet, sticky things.

Blood-sucking flies like mosquitoes and tsetse flies carry diseases such as malaria, yellow fever and sleeping sickness. They can infect humans when they pierce the skin with their mouth parts.

A fly defecates every four and a half minutes as it wanders across a beefburger.

Wing

Veins

Hind-gut

Abdomen

Heart

Mid-gut

Haltere

Crop

Thorax

Spiracle

Fore-gut

Trachea

Cerebral ganglion

Head

Compound eye

Esophagus

Flight muscle

Ganglion of nerve cord

Seta

Palp

Proboscis

Ommatidium

Pharynx

length = .5 inch (12 mm) house-fly

The fly's agility is due to its multi-jointed legs and the foot pads that let it walk on ceilings. Hairs on its legs act as sense organs and it has taste buds in its feet.

Femur

Spine

Leg joints

Tibia

Setae

Tarsi

Arolium

Tarsal claw

length = .25 inch sheep-ked (6.5 mm)

The sheep-ked is a wingless, permanently attached parasite of sheep.

length = .5 inch dung-fly (13 mm)

Dung-flies swarm around fresh dung, using it for food and as a place to lay eggs.

length = .5 inch parasitic fly (12 mm)

The larvae of parasitic flies live inside the bodies of insects and spiders.

length = .5 inch cattle-fly (12 mm)

The cattle-fly's powerful "beak" stabs its prey, giving it blood to drink.

length = 1 inch robber-fly (24 mm)

The robber-fly is a strong and fast flier that catches insects on the wing.

Ocellus

Orbit

Frons

ATRUE FLY IS AN INSECT with two wings. Many other insects are called flies, but closer examination reveals that they have four wings, not two. In the fly the second pair of wings is modified to form club-shaped stabilizers called halteres, or balancers. These are important for flying straight and level, something that the fly can do very well. Indeed, flies could be said to be the best aeronauts in the world. They can dart forwards, sideways, up and down, all in a matter of seconds. Flies can even land upside-down on the ceiling.

Over 90,000 species of fly have been recorded from all kinds of habitats the world over. These insects have exploited a wide range of food materials, ranging from blood, nectar and pollen, to rotting meat, fungi and dung. Several species hunt and catch other insects, while others are parasites as adults or larvae.

The bulging eyes of a fly are made up of thousands of tiny lenses, giving the fly good, all-round vision. They are particularly sensitive to movement - the fly can see the swat coming and can escape.

Flies and other insects see colors, some of which are invisible to humans.

Lens

Antenna

Face

Larvae

Egg

Flies might have disgusting habits, but they are very important in nature. Batches of up to 150 eggs are laid on corpses. Eggs hatch into maggots which burrow in and feed, so tidying up dead animals. Maggots turn into pupae, which hatch into flies.

Arista

Jowl

Palp

Proboscis

The housefly has remarkable eating habits; it dribbles saliva down its long proboscis onto food, to digest it. The resulting juices are soaked up by spongy lips and drawn into its mouth. As the female fly eats, she may lay eggs on the food. These hatch into maggots, which, in turn, feed on the food. A scrap of meat left out can become "fly-blown," crawling with maggots, very quickly.

Labella

length = .25 inch (6 mm) mosquito

length = .5 inch (12 mm) bee-fly

length = .15 inch (3 mm) fungus gnat

length = .5 inch (10 mm)

length = 1.5 inch (38 mm) crane-fly

antler-fly

The needle-like mouth parts of the female mosquito can pierce skin.

Easily mistaken for a bee, the bee-fly mimic lays its eggs near bees' nests.

The delicate fungus gnat, seen dancing in woods, has larvae which feed on fungi.

Long-legged crane-flies spend most of their lives as maggots.

The "antlers" of the antler fly carry eyes and are used by males to court females.

Rectum

Ejaculatory duct

Testis

Hind-leg

Folded wing

Wing veins

Cacae

Hind-gut

Heart

Mid-gut

THE FLY
AND OTHER
INSECTS

THERE ARE OVER A MILLION
KINDS of insect in the world today. Insects are
classed as invertebrates because, unlike fish,
mammals and birds they have no backbone.
The word insect means "cut into." Insects were given
their name because their bodies are cut, or divided, into
three parts. The head carries the brain, mouth parts and sense
organs, including eyes and antennas. The middle part, the thorax,
is where the three pairs of legs (and also the wings, if the insect has
them) are fixed. The rear part, the abdomen, contains most of the
intestines and other organs. Insects have a skeleton on the outside of their
body. The exoskeleton, made of a tough material
called chitin, supports, protects and gives
the insect strong limbs.

Malpighian tubules

Tracheole

Elytron

Tracheal trunk

Trachea

Muscles

Nerve

Arthrodial membrane

Tarsal claw

Abdominal ganglion

Tibia

Spine

Leg muscles of joints

Tarsal joints

Femur

Caterpillar to butterfly

Most insects go through
metamorphosis during their
development into an adult.

Metamorphosis means a
change of body form and
appearance.

Caterpillar

Chrysalis
(pupa)

Imago

wingspan = 1 inch

The development of a
butterfly, from egg to flying
insect, is a complex process
that involves several
distinct stages.

length = .4 inch (9 mm)
mining bee

Eggs hatch into caterpillars,
which shed their skin as
they grow. Each one then
changes into a chrysalis,
and a butterfly emerges.

Powerful wing muscles and
cleverly designed hinges
operate the wings of a butterfly.
The patterned wings also act as a
disguise or as a warning to predators.

European
swallow-tail
butterfly

length = .6 inch (15 mm)
African army ant

length = 1.5 inches
(36 mm)

length = 1 inch (27 mm)

grasshopper

ground beetle

In a tropical forest a colony of
army ants moves around its
territory, collecting food.

Not all bees live in hives.
Mining bees burrow into soil
and into the mortar
between bricks.

Enlarged back legs give
grasshoppers the power to
leap large distances. They
are related to the destructive
locust.

Ground beetles are active
hunters that search out and
eat other insects, slugs and
other small creatures.

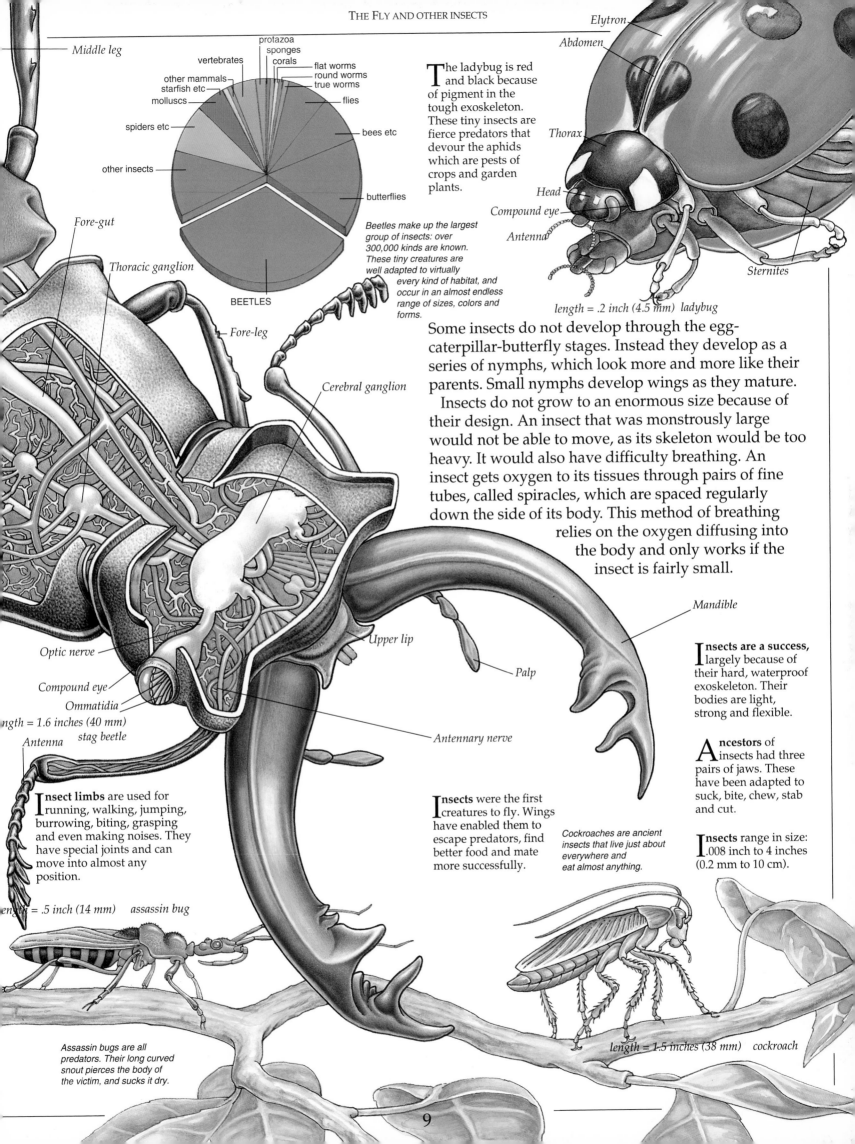

Middle leg

protazoa
sponges
corals
vertebrates
flat worms
other mammals
starfish etc
round worms
true worms
molluscs
flies
spiders etc
bees etc
other insects
butterflies
BEETLES

The ladybug is red and black because of pigment in the tough exoskeleton. These tiny insects are fierce predators that devour the aphids which are pests of crops and garden plants.

Elytron
Abdomen
Thorax
Head
Compound eye
Antenna
Sternites

length = .2 inch (4.5 mm) ladybug

Beetles make up the largest group of insects: over 300,000 kinds are known. These tiny creatures are well adapted to virtually every kind of habitat, and occur in an almost endless range of sizes, colors and forms.

Fore-gut

Thoracic ganglion

Fore-leg

Cerebral ganglion

Optic nerve

Compound eye

Ommatidia

length = 1.6 inches (40 mm) stag beetle

Antenna

Upper lip

Palp

Antennary nerve

Mandible

Some insects do not develop through the egg-caterpillar-butterfly stages. Instead they develop as a series of nymphs, which look more and more like their parents. Small nymphs develop wings as they mature.

Insects do not grow to an enormous size because of their design. An insect that was monstrously large would not be able to move, as its skeleton would be too heavy. It would also have difficulty breathing. An insect gets oxygen to its tissues through pairs of fine tubes, called spiracles, which are spaced regularly down the side of its body. This method of breathing relies on the oxygen diffusing into the body and only works if the insect is fairly small.

Insects are a success, largely because of their hard, waterproof exoskeleton. Their bodies are light, strong and flexible.

Ancestors of insects had three pairs of jaws. These have been adapted to suck, bite, chew, stab and cut.

Insects range in size: .008 inch to 4 inches (0.2 mm to 10 cm).

Insect limbs are used for running, walking, jumping, burrowing, biting, grasping and even making noises. They have special joints and can move into almost any position.

Insects were the first creatures to fly. Wings have enabled them to escape predators, find better food and mate more successfully.

Cockroaches are ancient insects that live just about everywhere and eat almost anything.

length = .5 inch (14 mm) assassin bug

Assassin bugs are all predators. Their long curved snout pierces the body of the victim, and sucks it dry.

length = 1.5 inches (38 mm) cockroach

9

Albumen gland   _Intestine_

Digestive gland

_Hermaphrodite
duct_

Kidney

Ovotestis

Mucus trail

Carrying their
homes on their
backs, snails are
found almost
anywhere. The snail's
body, including its
intestines, is twisted
in a spiral inside its
shell, either to the left
or to the right.

Stomach

The muscles of the
snails' foot
contract in ripples
from front to back.

Columella

Heart

Shell

The muscular "foot"
has glands that
make a slime of mucus
through which
the animal slithers.

The world's largest land snail was found in
Sierra Leone in 1976 and weighed 2 lbs
(900 g). Introduced into other parts of the world,
it became a pest, but is now under control by
another snail, from Florida, which eats it.

length = 1.2 inches (30 mm) garden snail

Papustyla _is a rare snail
that lives only in the
north of the Pacific
island of New Britain._

Rhynchotrochus _is a
little snail from Irian
Jaya that comes in 40
different forms._

Spermoviduct

Megalacron novaegeorgensis
creta, _a small snail from Papua
New Guinea, comes in three
colors - this is the rarest._

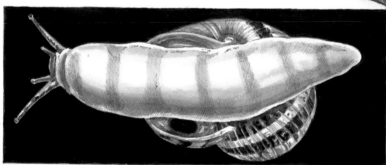

length = 6.5 inches (160 mm)   _length = 2 inches (45 mm)_

African giant snail   _Papustyla hindei_

length = 1 inch (28 mm)

_Rhynchotrochus
taylorianus_

_length = 1 inch (24 mm)
Megalacron novaegeorgensis
creta (pale form)_

THE SNAIL

garden snail

Stalked eye

SNAILS BELONG TO A DIVERSE and strange group of animals, the molluscs. This group contains over 80,000 species as different as the mussel and the octopus. All are soft-bodied with a visceral mass containing the main body organs that is covered by a sheet of tissue called the mantle. Beneath the visceral mass is the foot. Many species have a protective shell.

Land snails belong to a class of animals called the gastropods. The word *gastropod* means "foot-stomach." The snail's foot contains several organs, including parts of the gut. Its long coiled intestine is tucked away in the spirals of the shell. At the shell entrance, from where the body extends, is a cavity through which the snail breathes and discharges its waste.

The snail has a pair of sensitive tentacles on its head which detect chemicals in the world around it. It rasps its food with a rough tongue called a radula.

A mollusc's shell has a horny outer layer reinforced with inner layers of calcium carbonate. Secretions of calcium carbonate from beneath the shell increase the thickness. Secretions at the edge increase the diameter.

Lung

Shell

Salivary gland

Crop

Mucus gland

Dart sac

Esophagus

The head of a snail carries a pair of eyes on the tips of stalks. The tentacles contain sense organs to "taste and smell."

Radula

Tentacle

Excretory pore   Anus   Foot   Vagina   Penis

Pedal gland

Many snails eat vegetable matter but some will use their rasping radula to drill into the shells of other snails to eat them.

Snails, and their cousins the slugs, which lack an external shell, can be pests. They eat large quantities of crops and are a particular nuisance when seedlings are just growing. In tropical areas some snails carry diseases such as liver-fluke and bilharzia and spread them to humans.

Huge numbers of Cerion uva, a tropical island snail, can cover areas of vegetation.

The thin-shelled Helixarion lives in the rain forest of New South Wales, Australia.

Megaspira ruschenbergiana, the land snail with the longest shell, lives in the forests of Brazil.

length = 1.2 inches (30 mm)
Cerion uva

length = 1.7 inches (42 mm)
Helixarion irion

length = 4 inches (95 mm)
Megaspira ruschenbergiana

length = 1 inch (25 mm)
Megalacron novaegeorgensis creta (three color form)

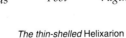

Mating snails

Dart sac

Vagina

Flagellum

Ovotestis

Albumen gland

Spermoviduct

Leopard cones are aggressive hunters that stab and poison their prey. They must be handled carefully.

length = 4 inches (100 mm)   leopard cone

The sex life of a snail is quite complicated. Many snails have both male and female sex organs (they are hermaphrodites). When two snails mate both become fertilized at the same time. This means that both snails become pregnant and produce young. Sex normally takes place after a complex courtship dance involving lots of circling and body contact.

During the late eighteenth and nineteenth centuries shell collecting became a very popular hobby. Because of this people learned a great deal about molluscs; they are, in fact, the fourth best known animal group, after mammals, birds and butterflies. Over 80,000 living species have been named, with a further 35,000 extinct species identified from fossils. Examples of extinct molluscs have been found in rocks that are 550 million years old.

Most squids are less than 8 inches (20 cm) long, but they can be 50 feet (17 m). The suckers of a 45-foot (15 m)-long squid leave 4-inch (10 cm) scars on whales, but whales have been found with 18-inch (45 cm) scars.

length = 50 feet (17 m)   giant squid

THE SNAIL AND OTHER
MOLLUSCS

MUSSELS, CLAMS, TUSK SHELLS, CHITONS, squids, octopuses and snails all belong to the mollusc group. All molluscs have a similar design, which usually includes a shell. While snails normally have only one shell, clams and oysters nestle between two hinged shells called valves. Chitons have eight overlapping shell plates, and the shell of a tusk shell is hollow. Many types of octopus and squid appear not to have a shell at all, but often have the remains of one hidden in their body.

A cuttlefish is a fast-moving, streamlined swimmer which is usually found in shallow waters. Its soft internal shell helps to keep it afloat in the water.

length = 1.3 inches (32 mm)
limpet

length = 3 inches (75 mm)
whelk

length = 1.2 inches (30 mm)
cockle

length = 3 inches (75 mm)
mussel

length = 16 inches (390 mm)   cuttlefish

length = 3.5inches (85 mm)   large black slug

Limpets cling tightly to rocks and graze on algae.

The whelk's long siphon finds the scent of a tasty corpse.

Cockles live in sand, feeding from the water above.

Special "golden" threads attach mussels to rocks.

The large black slug is a land gastropod that no longer has an external shell.

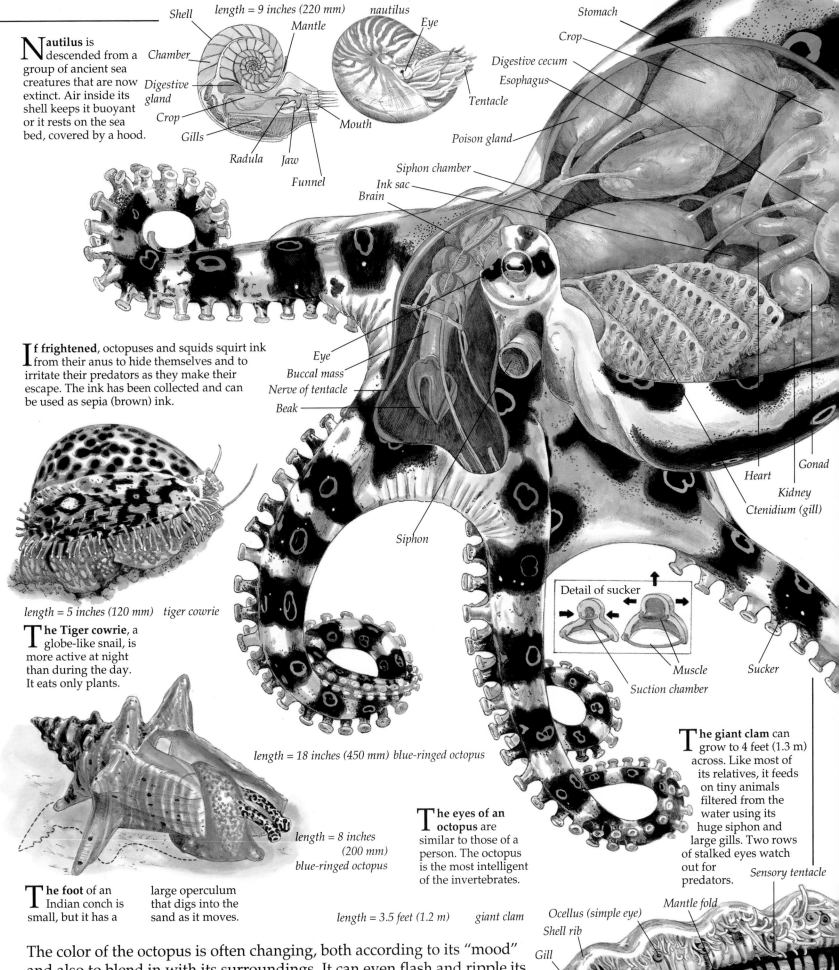

Nautilus is descended from a group of ancient sea creatures that are now extinct. Air inside its shell keeps it buoyant or it rests on the sea bed, covered by a hood.

length = 9 inches (220 mm)

Shell

Mantle

nautilus

Eye

Chamber

Digestive gland

Crop

Radula

Jaw

Funnel

Mouth

Tentacle

Stomach

Crop

Digestive cecum

Esophagus

Poison gland

Siphon chamber

Ink sac

Brain

Eye

Buccal mass

Nerve of tentacle

Beak

Siphon

Heart

Gonad

Kidney

Ctenidium (gill)

If **frightened**, octopuses and squids squirt ink from their anus to hide themselves and to irritate their predators as they make their escape. The ink has been collected and can be used as sepia (brown) ink.

length = 5 inches (120 mm)   tiger cowrie

The **Tiger cowrie**, a globe-like snail, is more active at night than during the day. It eats only plants.

length = 18 inches (450 mm) blue-ringed octopus

Detail of sucker

Muscle

Suction chamber

Sucker

The **giant clam** can grow to 4 feet (1.3 m) across. Like most of its relatives, it feeds on tiny animals filtered from the water using its huge siphon and large gills. Two rows of stalked eyes watch out for predators.

Sensory tentacle

The **foot** of an Indian conch is small, but it has a large operculum that digs into the sand as it moves.

length = 8 inches (200 mm) blue-ringed octopus

The **eyes of an octopus** are similar to those of a person. The octopus is the most intelligent of the invertebrates.

length = 3.5 feet (1.2 m)   giant clam

Ocellus (simple eye)

Shell rib

Gill

Mantle fold

The color of the octopus is often changing, both according to its "mood" and also to blend in with its surroundings. It can even flash and ripple its color patterns.

Squids and octopuses swim in similar ways. Squids move very fast by water propulsion - muscles force water out of the funnel, so that they are almost jet-propelled. Octopuses do not move as fast; they also use their arms to pull them along.

THE FROG

length = 4 inches (100 mm) common frog

The frog renews its tough outer layer of skin by molting.

Powerful, long back legs, attached to a large and strong pelvis, allow a frog to jump nearly 3.3 feet (1 m). Its short, stout front legs, firmly fixed to strong shoulders, take the shock of landing. In water, the frog's long webbed toes form broad paddles and make it an excellent swimmer. Some frogs have less webbing between their toes but have disc-like suckers on the underside of their feet that enable them to climb trees.

FROGS ARE PROBABLY the most successful of all amphibians. They are found all over the world except in the south of South America, most oceanic islands and in New Zealand. They live in damp places - marshes and ponds - and prey on insects, worms and slugs using a sticky tongue, attached to the front of their mouth. The tongue, which flips out very quickly, catches the unsuspecting victim before it has a chance to escape. The frog pushes the tasty morsel down its throat with its eyeballs, which move down forcefully as it blinks.

Brain

Nostril

Inner ear

Spinal cord

Mouth

Sacral vertebrae

Vertebrae

Eye

Urostyle

Kidney

Vas deferens

When a frog is sitting in water all that shows above the surface are its large bulging eyes. It watches warily for predators.

Tympanum of ear

Humerus

Heart

Cloaca

Stomach

Femur

Lung

Rectum

Small intestine

Testis

Epidermis

Mucus gland

Dermis

Toads have many poison glands in their skin. This is a defense against predators. Poisons produced by some toads can irritate your eyes and nose. One Colombian species has a venom that can kill if injected.

Mucus and poison glands excrete their contents onto the skin's surface, keeping it moist.

Blood vessel

Tadpoles and adult frogs and toads are omnivorous; they eat food that comes from both plants and animals.

Leg muscles

Tibia

Toe

Calcaneum   Astragalus

Webbing

One of the problems of living on land is that of breathing. Animals that live in water all the time can breathe through their skin, but respiration through the skin does not work well in air. Amphibians have developed lungs, which are used for breathing when the animals are not submerged in water.

length = 4.5 inches (110 mm) female smooth newt, walking

Amphibians show a remarkable range of color, produced by three layers of pigment cells in their skin that can expand to cause color changes. Some frogs and toads are well camouflaged while others are brightly colored to warn predators that they are poisonous. If frightened, a frog can startle its attacker by exposing highly colored patches on its legs as it jumps away.

Most frogs and toads lay their eggs in water as spawn. The tiny developing tadpoles are protected inside a thick jelly-like coat. On hatching, tadpoles have external gills that are gradually lost as internal gills and lungs grow. Their tail shortens and the tadpoles begin to look like adult frogs or toads.

Frog or toad? Frogs have smooth, wet skin; toads have dry, bumpy skin.

Over 2,600 different species of frog and toad are known today. The ancestors of present-day frogs were the first backboned animals to live on land. After 300 million years of evolution they are still bound to the aquatic life. Most return to the water to breed.

European green toad

length = 3.5 inches (90 mm)

European green toads live in the east of Europe and in the area from North Africa across to central Asia. These large nocturnal toads can be seen beneath street lamps in towns where they catch insects attracted to the light. Recent studies suggest that many species of frogs and toads are becoming rare, possibly because of pollution.

length = 5 inches (120 mm)   *edible frog*

Tongue

Phalanges

Jaw bones

Cranium

Humerus

Scapula

Vertebrae

Ileum

Phalanges

Metacarpals

Urostyle

Carpals

Radius

Femur

Ulna

Tibia

Frogs and toads are tailless amphibians with a peculiar skeleton designed for jumping and swimming. Weak jaws in a fish-like skull prevent them from eating tough or very active prey.

Ischium

Astragalus

Phalanges

Calcaneum

Distal tarsals

Tarsals

THE FROG AND OTHER
AMPHIBIANS

length = 6 inches
(150 mm)
caecilian

FROGS, TOADS, NEWTS, SALAMANDERS AND CAECILIANS are all amphibians. As the name suggests (*amphi* for "both" and *bios* for "life") they can live in water or on land. They tend to live in the water when young and out of it when adult and are tied to water far more than reptiles and mammals. In many ways they are very fish-like, with their weak skulls and their need for water in which to lay their eggs.

Salamanders and newts all have a tail; they have a fish-like skeleton, and look like a wriggling fish as they walk. Their legs stick out from their body, and as their feet touch the ground they are turned forwards. Although these limbs allow the animals to move around, they are not as efficient as proper legs placed firmly underneath the body. As a salamander walks, its stomach is dragged along the ground, squashing the organs inside that are not protected by ribs.

Eye

Head

Pectoral girdle

Humerus

Frogs and toads make all manner of croaks, squeaks, bubbles and grunts to attract females, and to mark out territory.

Ulna

Radius

Phalanges

Wrist bones

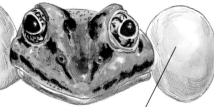

Blind, limbless, long-bodied caecilians are found in the tropics; they burrow in soil to search for worms to eat.

When a frog croaks, air is pumped back and forth through vocal cords between the lungs and one or more vocal pouches. The vocal pouches swell and act as resonators like the body of a guitar.

Air sac

length = 7 inches (180 mm)   axolotl

length = 7 inches (175 mm)
Colombian horned frog

The axolotl is a salamander that looks like an overgrown tadpole. It even has feathery gills like a tadpole. This larval form is kept throughout the axolotl's life, and it breeds in this form.

With its huge head and wide gape, the Colombian horned frog can eat other frogs whole.

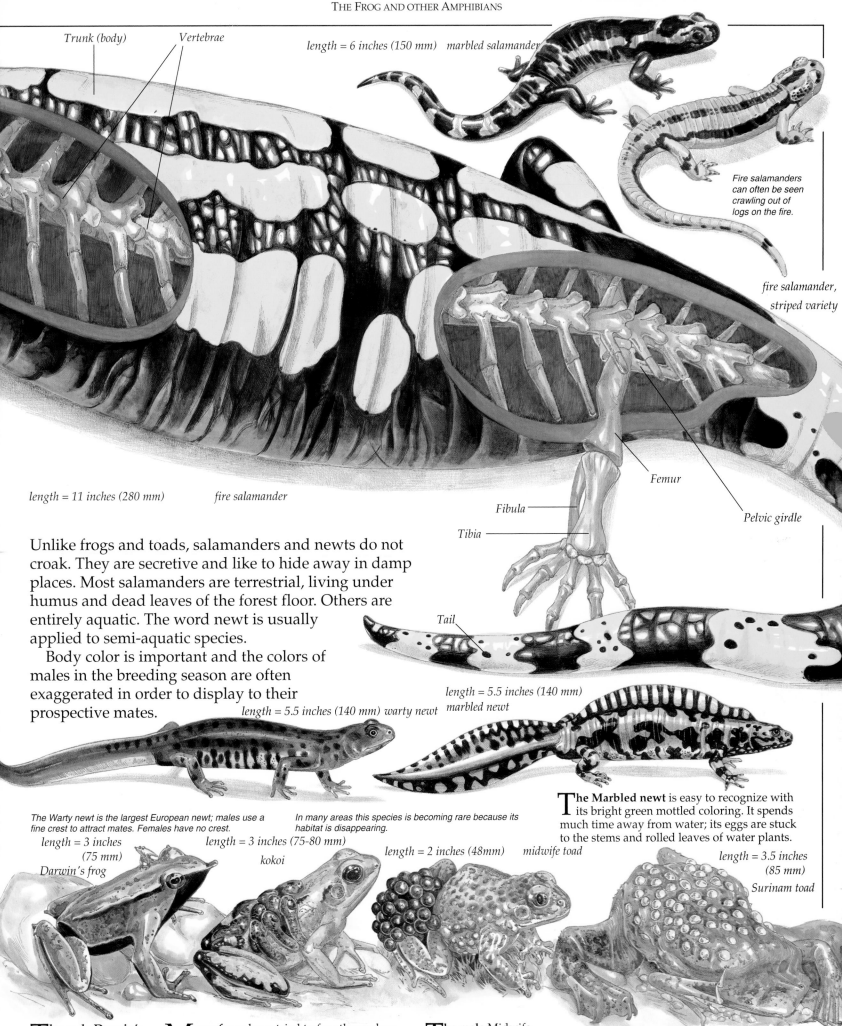

Trunk (body)

Vertebrae

length = 6 inches (150 mm)   marbled salamander

Fire salamanders can often be seen crawling out of logs on the fire.

fire salamander, striped variety

length = 11 inches (280 mm)   fire salamander

Femur

Pelvic girdle

Fibula

Tibia

Unlike frogs and toads, salamanders and newts do not croak. They are secretive and like to hide away in damp places. Most salamanders are terrestrial, living under humus and dead leaves of the forest floor. Others are entirely aquatic. The word newt is usually applied to semi-aquatic species.

Body color is important and the colors of males in the breeding season are often exaggerated in order to display to their prospective mates.

Tail

length = 5.5 inches (140 mm) marbled newt

length = 5.5 inches (140 mm) warty newt

The Marbled newt is easy to recognize with its bright green mottled coloring. It spends much time away from water; its eggs are stuck to the stems and rolled leaves of water plants.

The Warty newt is the largest European newt; males use a fine crest to attract mates. Females have no crest.

In many areas this species is becoming rare because its habitat is disappearing.

length = 3 inches (75 mm)
Darwin's frog

length = 3 inches (75-80 mm)
kokoi

length = 2 inches (48mm)   midwife toad

length = 3.5 inches (85 mm)
Surinam toad

The male Darwin's frog has an odd way to carry tadpoles - in its vocal sac.

Many frogs have tried to free themselves from water. The tadpoles of the Kokoi frog are carried by their father on his back. He dips them in water to keep their skin wet.

The male Midwife toad carries eggs, laid by the female, for a month before hatching.

The Surinam toad is a tongueless water toad; eggs are embedded in the female's back.

THE FISH

length = 12 inches (300 mm) perch

Fish are vertebrates, which means that they have a backbone and an internal skeleton rather than an external or outside "shell." There are five main groups of vertebrates: fish, amphibians, reptiles, birds and mammals. Of these, fish were the first to evolve, arising over 500 million years ago.

Most fish live in water, breathe through gills, have a scaly body, and swim and maneuver themselves about using fins. Fish are cold-blooded. There are 20,000 kinds or species of fish living in the sea, and 5,000 in rivers, lakes and ponds. Some, such as salmon, eels and sturgeon, move between the sea and fresh water.

Fish eyes are raised and face sideways, and can see in all directions.

Sound vibrations traveling through the water, which are caused by movements, are picked up by the lateral line, which runs along each side of the body.

The jaws and teeth of different kinds of fish are adapted to eating different foods.

Dorsal fin

Basal fin support

Dorsal crest of skull

Vertebrae

Swim bladder

Rib

Eye

Nostrils

Teeth

Mouth

Dentary

A thick, muscular body lets the fish swim continuously.

Gill arch   Articular   Branchiostegal rays   Opercular bones   Liver

Pyloric appendices

Pelvic fin

Most fish have the same basic structure, but they have become adapted to their own habitat. Some swim continuously in the open ocean and are streamlined and sleek. Others nose around on the seabed and are broad and squat. Large powerful tail fins are used for speed, and tiny delicate fins are for gently weaving in and out of seaweeds. Vicious teeth chew other fish and small, tubular mouths suck in tiny shrimps. Muddy colors hide a fish among rotting leaves in a tropical stream, while brilliantly colored fish live among the poisonous tentacles of sea anemones.

Under each gill cover are four gills with a double row of gill filaments on each, which will absorb oxygen. The gill cover or operculum controls the passage of water out of the body.

The front and back fins propel fish through water. They often have bony rods inside them for support and strength.

large mouth bass
length= 3.3 feet (1 m)

inconu

length = 9.5 inches (240 mm)

roach

Roach live in deep water in slow-flowing cool streams and lakes.

Trout love fresh water but they can also live in the sea.

trout

length = 15 inches (380 mm)

The Inconu is a white fish with bristle-like teeth and is found in Arctic waters.

length= 10 inches (250 mm)

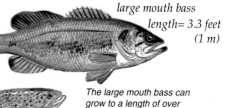

The large mouth bass can grow to a length of over 6.7 feet (2 m).

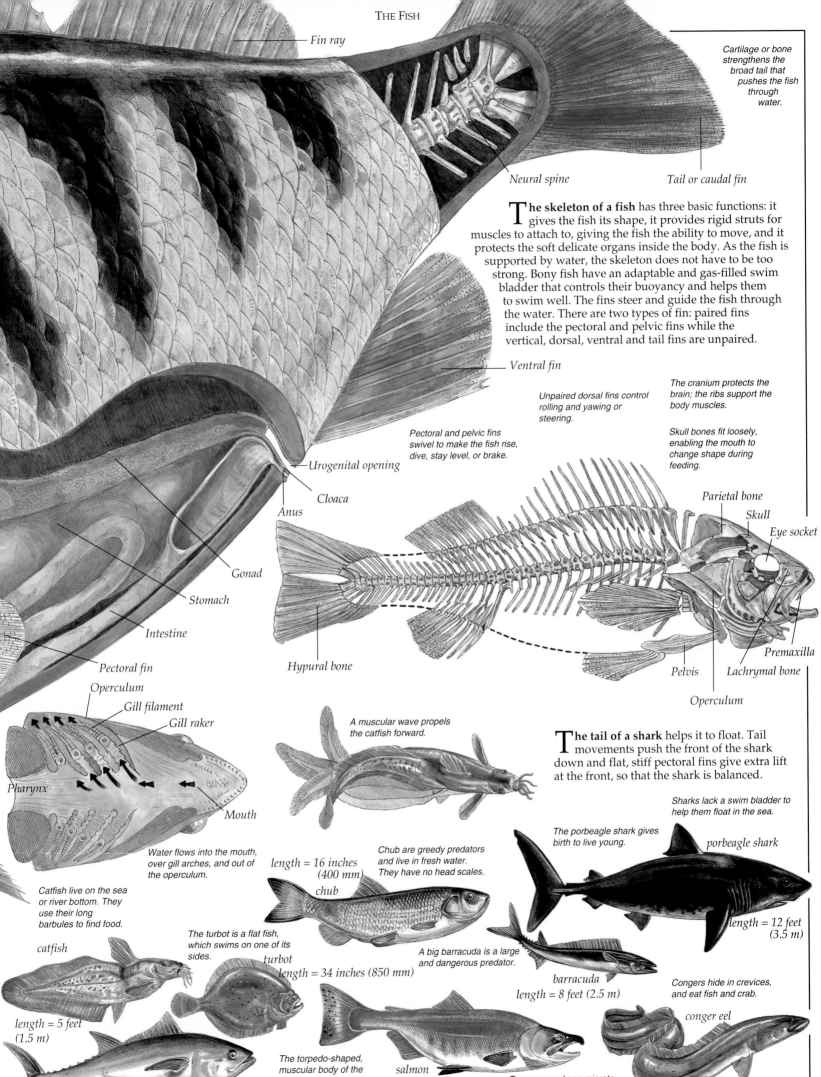

Fin ray

Cartilage or bone strengthens the broad tail that pushes the fish through water.

Neural spine

Tail or caudal fin

The skeleton of a fish has three basic functions: it gives the fish its shape, it provides rigid struts for muscles to attach to, giving the fish the ability to move, and it protects the soft delicate organs inside the body. As the fish is supported by water, the skeleton does not have to be too strong. Bony fish have an adaptable and gas-filled swim bladder that controls their buoyancy and helps them to swim well. The fins steer and guide the fish through the water. There are two types of fin: paired fins include the pectoral and pelvic fins while the vertical, dorsal, ventral and tail fins are unpaired.

Ventral fin

Unpaired dorsal fins control rolling and yawing or steering.

The cranium protects the brain; the ribs support the body muscles.

Pectoral and pelvic fins swivel to make the fish rise, dive, stay level, or brake.

Skull bones fit loosely, enabling the mouth to change shape during feeding.

Urogenital opening

Cloaca

Anus

Gonad

Stomach

Intestine

Pectoral fin

Operculum

Gill filament

Gill raker

Pharynx

Mouth

Parietal bone

Skull

Eye socket

Premaxilla

Lachrymal bone

Pelvis

Operculum

Hypural bone

Water flows into the mouth, over gill arches, and out of the operculum.

A muscular wave propels the catfish forward.

The tail of a shark helps it to float. Tail movements push the front of the shark down and flat, stiff pectoral fins give extra lift at the front, so that the shark is balanced.

Sharks lack a swim bladder to help them float in the sea.

Catfish live on the sea or river bottom. They use their long barbules to find food.

length = 16 inches (400 mm)

chub

Chub are greedy predators and live in fresh water. They have no head scales.

The porbeagle shark gives birth to live young.

porbeagle shark

catfish

The turbot is a flat fish, which swims on one of its sides.

turbot

length = 34 inches (850 mm)

A big barracuda is a large and dangerous predator.

barracuda

length = 8 feet (2.5 m)

length = 12 feet (3.5 m)

Congers hide in crevices, and eat fish and crab.

conger eel

length = 5 feet (1.5 m)

The torpedo-shaped, muscular body of the southern bluefin tuna makes it one of the fastest ocean fish.

salmon

length = 18 inches (450 mm)

To spawn, salmon migrate from the sea to rivers where they were born.

length = 6.7 feet (2 m)

bluefin tuna

length = 14 feet (4.3 m)

FEROCIOUS FISH

SHARKS ARE ALL HIGHLY ADAPTED attacking and killing machines. They detect prey with finely tuned senses - they have excellent eyesight, a good sense of smell and sensitive electricity-detecting organs that can easily locate moving prey. They also have wide, gaping jaws and razor-sharp teeth for catching and eating their victims. Their teeth can be large or small, thin and pointed or triangular and blade-like depending on the species. Different sharks have teeth adapted for catching different types of prey.

However, not all sharks are the streamlined, active predators familiar to us from adventure films; there are also some slow-moving, slightly less fierce species that are rounder and not as sleek.

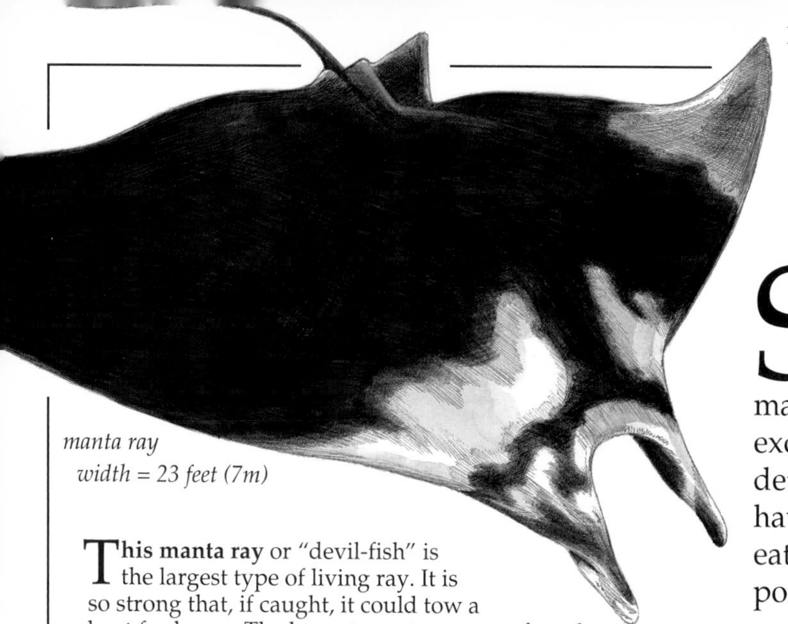

manta ray
width = 23 feet (7m)

This manta ray or "devil-fish" is the largest type of living ray. It is so strong that, if caught, it could tow a boat for hours. The largest manta ray ever found measured 23 feet (7 m) across and weighed two tons. Despite their ferocious appearance and wide mouths, mantas have small teeth and are gentle plankton-eaters. The fleshy lobes on either side of the mouth channel water over the gills, and the plankton is filtered off.

Sharks will attack penguins, birds, seals, dolphins, crabs, squid and even other sharks. Their teeth are continuously replaced and there may be more than one row in a shark's mouth at one time.

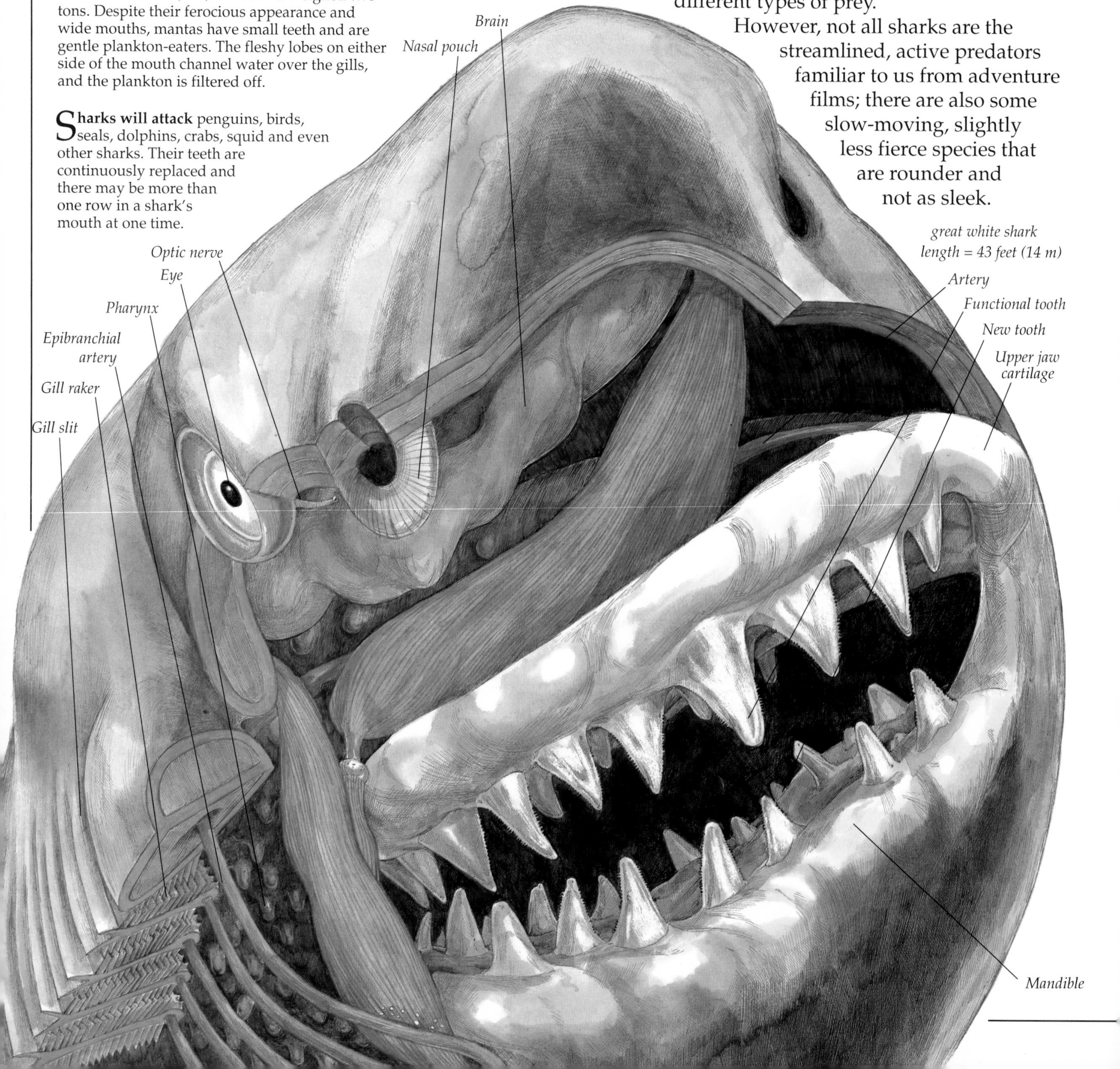

great white shark
length = 43 feet (14 m)

Brain
Nasal pouch
Optic nerve
Eye
Pharynx
Epibranchial artery
Gill raker
Gill slit
Artery
Functional tooth
New tooth
Upper jaw cartilage
Mandible

A **sea horse** is a strange kind of fish. Its head is bent so that it looks like a horse, and it has an armored body and a prehensile tail. Its tiny dorsal fin ripples like a propeller as the sea horse moves in and out of the weeds.

length = 4.5 inches (110 mm)

sea horse

D **ressed to look like a mass of seaweed**, the sea dragon is well camouflaged. Like other sea horses it creeps up on small shrimps and sucks them into its mouth like a vacuum cleaner.

sea dragon
length = 5 inches (120 mm)

While most other fish have bony skeletons, sharks and rays have a skeleton of soft cartilage. They occur in many different shapes, colors and sizes. From above they usually appear dark and dull, blending in with their background of weed and the seabed. From below they are shiny with a much lighter coloring. This allows them to camouflage themselves against the ripples and sparkles of the water. This counter-shading helps them to avoid being seen by predators.

The scorpion fish is brightly colored and hides among rocks, waiting for prey. The spiny rays in its fins house glands that make a powerful poison.

scorpion fish
length = 12 inches (300 mm)

flying fish

Large pectoral fins make it possible for "flying" fish to glide.

length = 10 inches (250 mm)

harlequin tusk fish
length = 9 inches (220 mm)

hatchet fish

length = 4 inches (100 mm)

Organs on the side of a hatchet fish give out light.

The electric field surrounding an electric eel.

When frightened, globefish fill themselves with air and make their spines stand out.

globe fish   *length = 10 inches (250mm)*

− +

Spine

Electric organ

The strange blue teeth of the Harlequin Tusk-fish can crunch crabs and shellfish.

electric eel   length = 9 inches (230 mm)

By sensing changes in their surrounding electric field several fish use electricity to find their way about and to detect prey. The amazing organ of the electric eel can generate over 500 volts.

O **rnamental fish** include the calico-veil and Koi carp. Many different forms of these and other fish give a great deal of pleasure to the people who keep them.

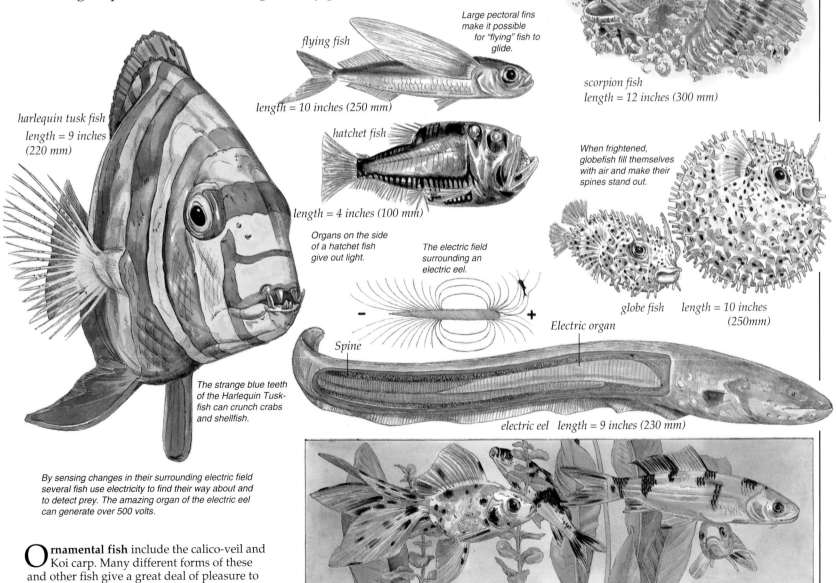

calico-veil goldfish length = 5 inches (120 mm)   *koi carp   length = 12 inches (300 mm)*

THE SNAKE

A large reticulated python that can grow to a length of 33 feet (10 m) can swallow a small deer or pig.

length = 26 feet (8 m)   *reticulated python*

The scales on a snake's head are much thicker and tougher than those on the rest of its body. The snake's head is narrow at the front and broad at the back. This makes it easy for the animal to push through foliage, burrow into soft soil and squeeze under rocks and logs.

Pupil

Nostril

Heart

Forked tongue

Scales

Snakes can see well and they have a good sense of smell. When a snake flicks out its forked tongue, it is "smelling" the air. The tongue picks up scent molecules and as it is drawn back into the mouth, the tip touches some special pits. The cells within these pits are very sensitive to smells and can tell the snake if prey or a predator is nearby.

Head scales
Orbit
Retina
Conus
Iris
Lens
Spectacle
Cornea

Certain snakes, including rattlesnakes, have a heat-sensitive pit between their nostrils and eyes, so they can stalk a warm-blooded rat, even in the dark. Not all snakes feed at night; some hunt during the day.

Gall bladder

Liver

Lung

Vitreous body

Sclerotic cup

Skin

Optic nerve

Stomach

SNAKES ARE PECULIAR LEGLESS REPTILES with long, slender bodies. It is thought that they have evolved from a kind of burrowing lizard that eventually lost its legs. Some snakes, such as boas and pythons, have the remains of hind legs, which still have claws. These are used in mating.

Slithering along on its belly, a snake has to protect its soft, vulnerable insides from being squashed. Heart, lungs, liver and intestines are all safe within a rib cage which extends to the tail. Snakes have between 180 and 400 vertebrae along their backbones. Being elongated has also affected the organs of the snake's body. The left lung is often very small and the blood system is also unequally developed, with far fewer blood vessels found in the left part of the body. Each snake vertebra fits against its neighbor in a special way that allows maximum sideways and downward movement but minimal upward flexibility. This prevents the body from binding in the wrong place when the snake moves.

Boas and pythons live in trees, have long bodies and feed mainly on mammals, which they suffocate by constriction. The snake wraps its body in coils around the victim and as the coils are tightened the prey is killed.

Snakes are not at all slimy, as most people think. The surface of a snake, which is smooth and dry, is covered in overlapping scales. These prevent too much moisture being lost through the skin.

Spine

Skull

Tail

Ribs

Vestigial pelvis

Lower jaw

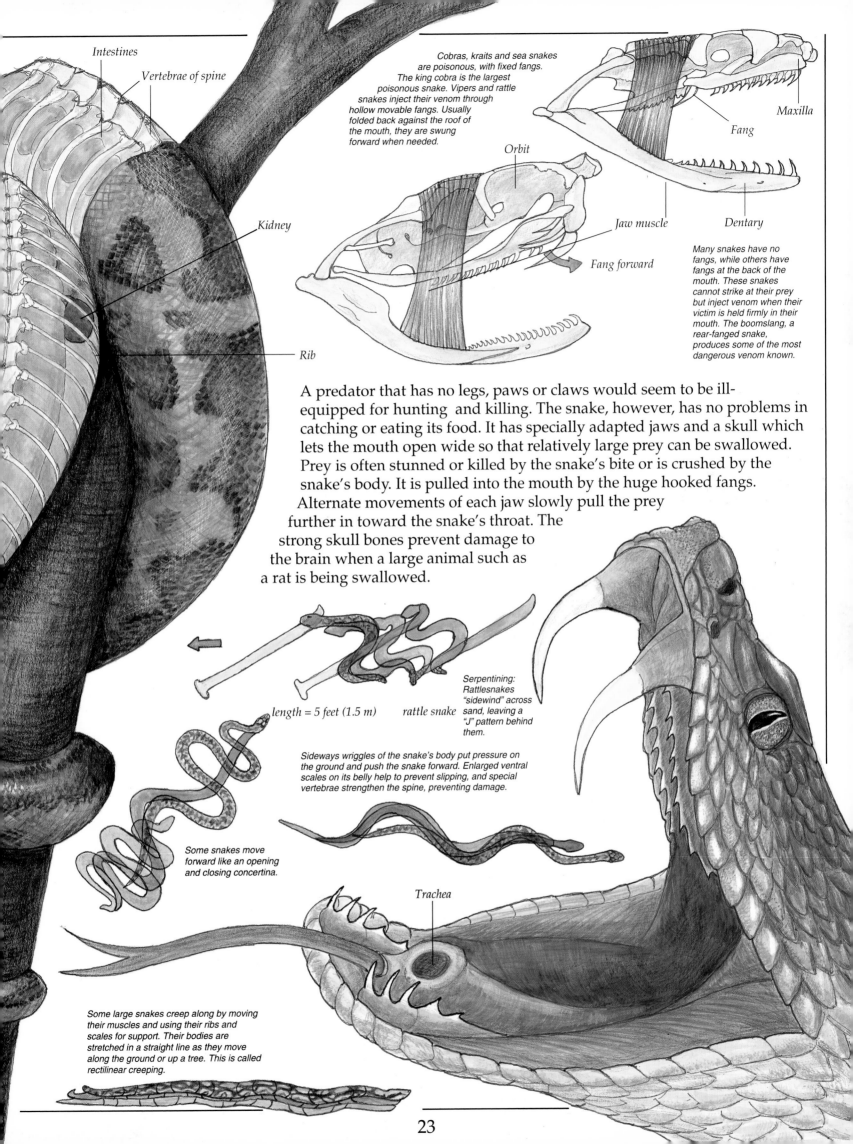

Intestines

Vertebrae of spine

Kidney

Rib

Cobras, kraits and sea snakes are poisonous, with fixed fangs. The king cobra is the largest poisonous snake. Vipers and rattle snakes inject their venom through hollow movable fangs. Usually folded back against the roof of the mouth, they are swung forward when needed.

Maxilla

Fang

Orbit

Jaw muscle

Dentary

Fang forward

Many snakes have no fangs, while others have fangs at the back of the mouth. These snakes cannot strike at their prey but inject venom when their victim is held firmly in their mouth. The boomslang, a rear-fanged snake, produces some of the most dangerous venom known.

A predator that has no legs, paws or claws would seem to be ill-equipped for hunting and killing. The snake, however, has no problems in catching or eating its food. It has specially adapted jaws and a skull which lets the mouth open wide so that relatively large prey can be swallowed. Prey is often stunned or killed by the snake's bite or is crushed by the snake's body. It is pulled into the mouth by the huge hooked fangs. Alternate movements of each jaw slowly pull the prey further in toward the snake's throat. The strong skull bones prevent damage to the brain when a large animal such as a rat is being swallowed.

length = 5 feet (1.5 m)   rattle snake

Serpentining: Rattlesnakes "sidewind" across sand, leaving a "J" pattern behind them.

Sideways wriggles of the snake's body put pressure on the ground and push the snake forward. Enlarged ventral scales on its belly help to prevent slipping, and special vertebrae strengthen the spine, preventing damage.

Some snakes move forward like an opening and closing concertina.

Trachea

Some large snakes creep along by moving their muscles and using their ribs and scales for support. Their bodies are stretched in a straight line as they move along the ground or up a tree. This is called rectilinear creeping.

Paddle-like limbs propel turtles effortlessly through water but force them to walk laboriously on land.

Phalanges

Radius

Ulna

Eye

Scapula

Vertebrae

Proscapula process

Pelvis

Tail

Centrum

Coracoid

Plastron

pond terrapin

length = 6 inches (150 mm)

In tortoises and turtles the shell is made up of 59–61 bones, and is in two parts: the plastron is underneath and covers the belly and the carapace forms the domed covering on top. The animal's vertebrae are fixed to the shell's inner surface. In stressful situations the turtle or tortoise can protect itself by pulling its legs, tail, head and neck right back inside the shell.

THE SNAKE AND OTHER
REPTILES

IN THE PAST, MANY DIFFERENT REPTILES roamed the Earth, but today only four groups exist. Lizards and snakes are members of the most successful group. The crocodiles are another group which has been around much longer than the snakes and lizards. Ancient ancestors of the crocodiles also evolved into birds. A living fossil, the tuatara, from New Zealand is the sole survivor of the third group, and the tortoises and turtles form the fourth group. These all have specially adapted shells and resemble some of the ancient, now extinct, reptiles.

Reptiles are cold-blooded vertebrates; they usually lay their eggs on land, have a scaly skin and can change their appearance to blend in with their natural background.

Vipers are ground-dwelling snakes with a short tail.

length = 6 feet (1.8 m)   gaboon viper

On the forest floor, vipers are hard to see.

Rings of red, black and yellow warn that the coral snake is very dangerous.

coral snake

length = 22 inches (560 mm)

When the cobra is frightened, it raises ribs behind its head into a "hood." It does so to seem fierce and intimidating.

length = 7 feet (2.2 m)   black cobra

length = 10 inches (250 mm) blind snake

Blind snakes are smooth and short-tailed, with round heads, and are good burrowers. Their eyes are small and useless

Crocodiles can eat and breathe at the same time because the roof of their mouth is a "false-palate."

A flap at the back of the tongue separates off the airway as the animal starts to swallow.

Crocodiles are the only reptiles that can do this.

Female crocodilians lay their eggs in pits in the sand by a water supply. When the eggs hatch, the female carries the young crocodiles to the water by picking them up and carrying them gently inside her mouth.

When a large animal is caught or found dead by the waterside, the crocodile will pull it into deeper water. It will then grasp a limb and violently rotate the body, spinning it, and so tearing it apart. The victim may not be eaten immediately, but hidden away in an underwater larder and eaten later.

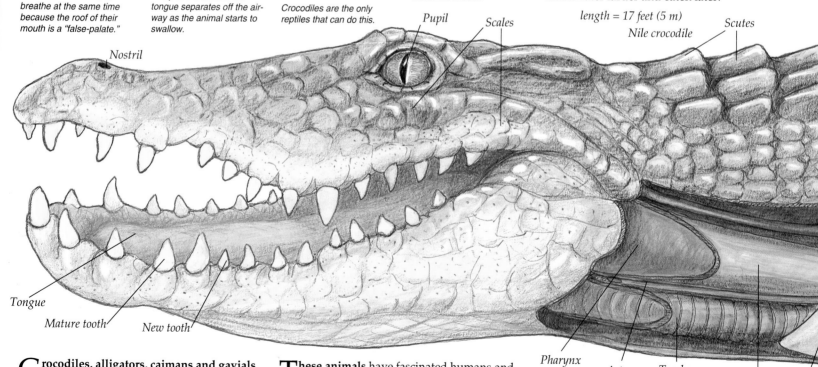

Pupil

Scales

length = 17 feet (5 m)

Scutes

Nile crocodile

Nostril

Tongue

Mature tooth

New tooth

Pharynx

Artery   Trachea

Esophagus

Coracoid

Crocodiles, alligators, caimans and gavials all have nostrils on the top of their head so that they can still breathe while partially submerged under the water.

These animals have fascinated humans and are often found in zoos. Crocodiles can live for an average 25 years in captivity. Alligators tend to live slightly longer; 35 years is average.

Some crocodilians can get very large. The American crocodile can grow to over 26 feet (7 m) and the gavial to 22 feet (6.5 m).

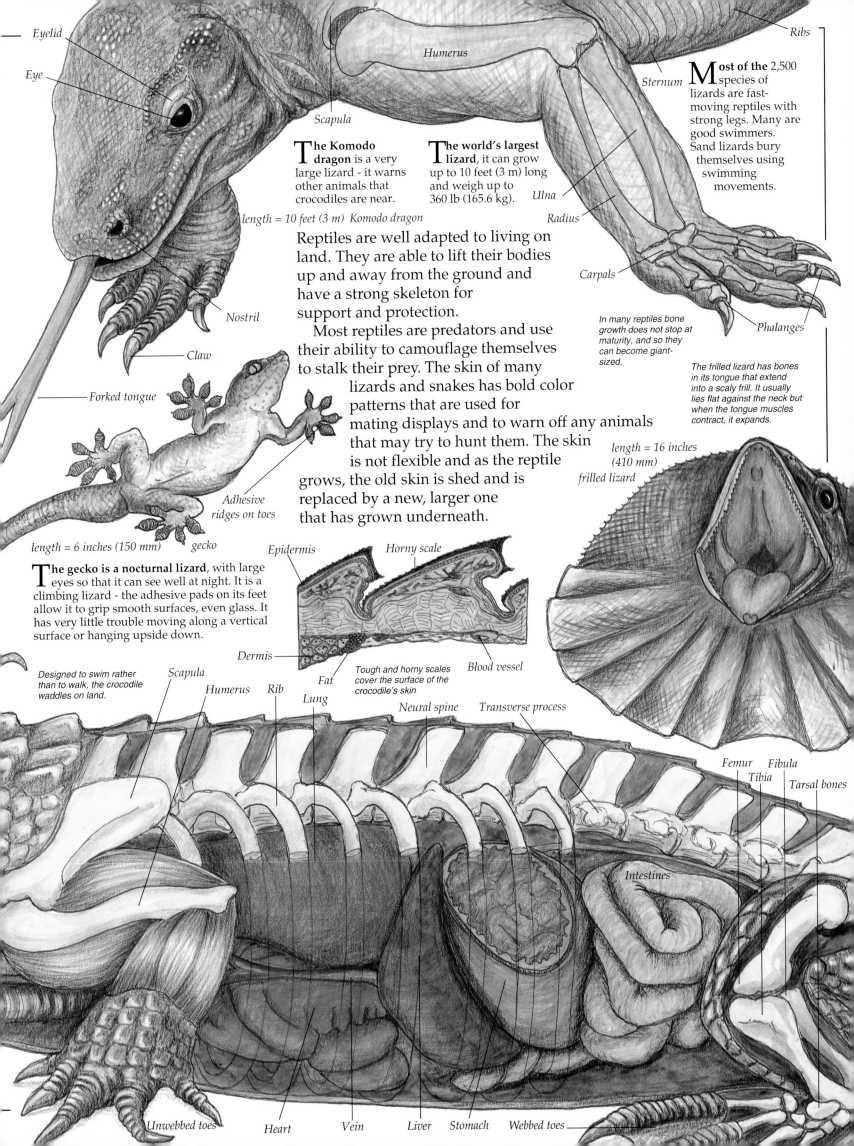

Eyelid

Eye

Humerus

Ribs

Scapula

Sternum

Most of the 2,500 species of lizards are fast-moving reptiles with strong legs. Many are good swimmers. Sand lizards bury themselves using swimming movements.

The Komodo dragon is a very large lizard - it warns other animals that crocodiles are near.

The world's largest lizard, it can grow up to 10 feet (3 m) long and weigh up to 360 lb (165.6 kg).

Ulna

Radius

length = 10 feet (3 m) Komodo dragon

Reptiles are well adapted to living on land. They are able to lift their bodies up and away from the ground and have a strong skeleton for support and protection.

Most reptiles are predators and use their ability to camouflage themselves to stalk their prey. The skin of many lizards and snakes has bold color patterns that are used for mating displays and to warn off any animals that may try to hunt them. The skin is not flexible and as the reptile grows, the old skin is shed and is replaced by a new, larger one that has grown underneath.

Carpals

Phalanges

In many reptiles bone growth does not stop at maturity, and so they can become giant-sized.

The frilled lizard has bones in its tongue that extend into a scaly frill. It usually lies flat against the neck but when the tongue muscles contract, it expands.

Nostril

Claw

Forked tongue

Adhesive ridges on toes

length = 16 inches (410 mm)

frilled lizard

length = 6 inches (150 mm)   gecko

The gecko is a nocturnal lizard, with large eyes so that it can see well at night. It is a climbing lizard - the adhesive pads on its feet allow it to grip smooth surfaces, even glass. It has very little trouble moving along a vertical surface or hanging upside down.

Epidermis

Horny scale

Dermis

Fat

Tough and horny scales cover the surface of the crocodile's skin

Blood vessel

Designed to swim rather than to walk, the crocodile waddles on land.

Scapula

Humerus

Rib

Lung

Neural spine

Transverse process

Femur *Fibula*

Tibia

Tarsal bones

Intestines

Unwebbed toes   *Heart*   *Vein*   *Liver*   *Stomach*   *Webbed toes*

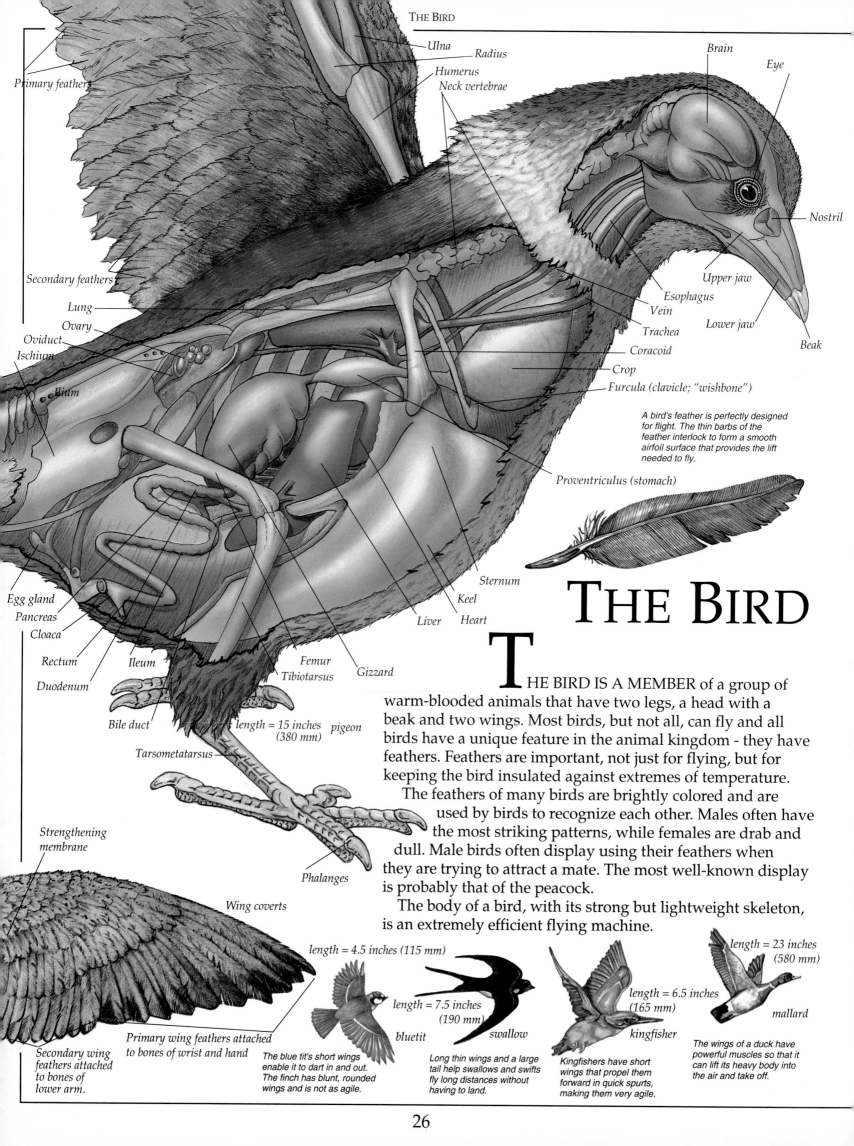

Ulna
Radius
Humerus
Neck vertebrae
Primary feathers
Brain
Eye
Nostril
Upper jaw
Esophagus
Vein
Trachea
Lower jaw
Beak
Secondary feathers
Lung
Ovary
Oviduct
Ischium
Ilium
Coracoid
Crop
Furcula (clavicle; "wishbone")

A bird's feather is perfectly designed for flight. The thin barbs of the feather interlock to form a smooth airfoil surface that provides the lift needed to fly.

Proventriculus (stomach)

Egg gland
Pancreas
Cloaca
Rectum
Ileum
Duodenum
Bile duct
Tarsometatarsus
Femur
Tibiotarsus
Gizzard
Sternum
Keel
Liver
Heart
length = 15 inches (380 mm)   pigeon

Strengthening membrane
Phalanges
Wing coverts

THE BIRD

THE BIRD IS A MEMBER of a group of warm-blooded animals that have two legs, a head with a beak and two wings. Most birds, but not all, can fly and all birds have a unique feature in the animal kingdom - they have feathers. Feathers are important, not just for flying, but for keeping the bird insulated against extremes of temperature.

The feathers of many birds are brightly colored and are used by birds to recognize each other. Males often have the most striking patterns, while females are drab and dull. Male birds often display using their feathers when they are trying to attract a mate. The most well-known display is probably that of the peacock.

The body of a bird, with its strong but lightweight skeleton, is an extremely efficient flying machine.

Secondary wing feathers attached to bones of lower arm.
Primary wing feathers attached to bones of wrist and hand

length = 4.5 inches (115 mm)

length = 7.5 inches (190 mm)

length = 6.5 inches (165 mm)

length = 23 inches (580 mm)

bluetit
swallow
kingfisher
mallard

The blue tit's short wings enable it to dart in and out. The finch has blunt, rounded wings and is not as agile.

Long thin wings and a large tail help swallows and swifts fly long distances without having to land.

Kingfishers have short wings that propel them forward in quick spurts, making them very agile.

The wings of a duck have powerful muscles so that it can lift its heavy body into the air and take off.

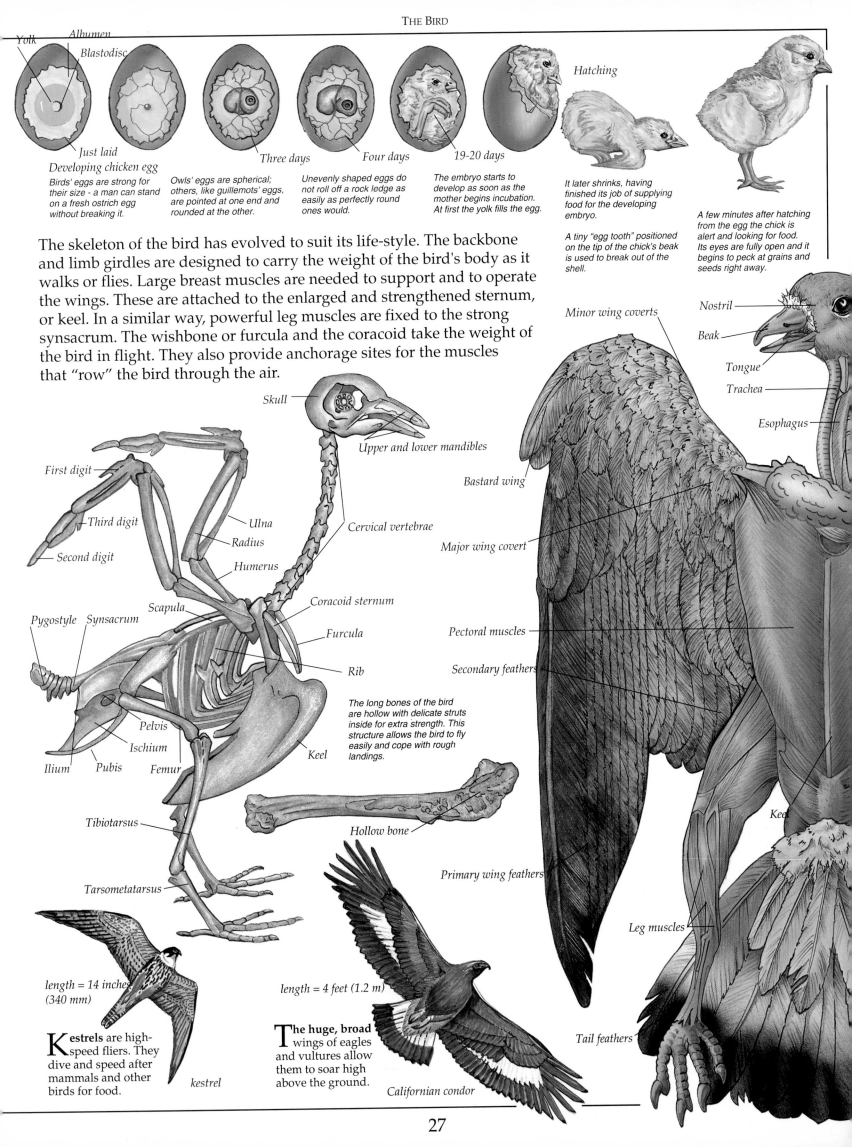

Yolk

Albumen

Blastodisc

Just laid

Developing chicken egg

Birds' eggs are strong for their size - a man can stand on a fresh ostrich egg without breaking it.

Three days

Owls' eggs are spherical; others, like guillemots' eggs, are pointed at one end and rounded at the other.

Four days

Unevenly shaped eggs do not roll off a rock ledge as easily as perfectly round ones would.

19-20 days

The embryo starts to develop as soon as the mother begins incubation. At first the yolk fills the egg.

Hatching

It later shrinks, having finished its job of supplying food for the developing embryo.

A tiny "egg tooth" positioned on the tip of the chick's beak is used to break out of the shell.

A few minutes after hatching from the egg the chick is alert and looking for food. Its eyes are fully open and it begins to peck at grains and seeds right away.

The skeleton of the bird has evolved to suit its life-style. The backbone and limb girdles are designed to carry the weight of the bird's body as it walks or flies. Large breast muscles are needed to support and to operate the wings. These are attached to the enlarged and strengthened sternum, or keel. In a similar way, powerful leg muscles are fixed to the strong synsacrum. The wishbone or furcula and the coracoid take the weight of the bird in flight. They also provide anchorage sites for the muscles that "row" the bird through the air.

Minor wing coverts

Nostril

Beak

Tongue

Trachea

Esophagus

Skull

Upper and lower mandibles

Bastard wing

Cervical vertebrae

Major wing covert

First digit

Third digit

Ulna

Radius

Second digit

Humerus

Pectoral muscles

Scapula

Coracoid sternum

Pygostyle Synsacrum

Furcula

Secondary feathers

Rib

The long bones of the bird are hollow with delicate struts inside for extra strength. This structure allows the bird to fly easily and cope with rough landings.

Pelvis

Ischium

Ilium Pubis Femur

Keel

Keel

Tibiotarsus

Hollow bone

Tarsometatarsus

Primary wing feathers

Leg muscles

length = 14 inches (340 mm)

length = 4 feet (1.2 m)

Tail feathers

Kestrels are high-speed fliers. They dive and speed after mammals and other birds for food.

kestrel

The huge, broad wings of eagles and vultures allow them to soar high above the ground.

Californian condor

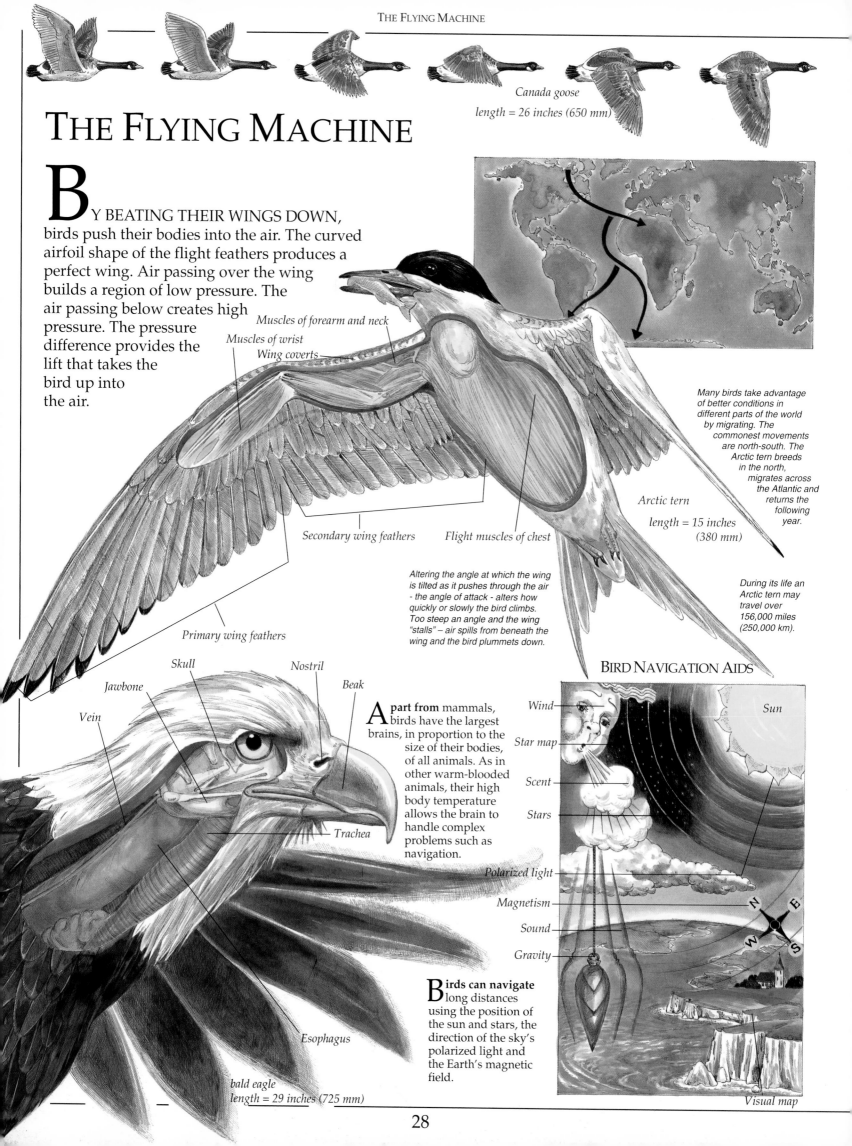

Canada goose
length = 26 inches (650 mm)

THE FLYING MACHINE

BY BEATING THEIR WINGS DOWN, birds push their bodies into the air. The curved airfoil shape of the flight feathers produces a perfect wing. Air passing over the wing builds a region of low pressure. The air passing below creates high pressure. The pressure difference provides the lift that takes the bird up into the air.

Muscles of forearm and neck

Muscles of wrist

Wing coverts

Secondary wing feathers

Flight muscles of chest

Primary wing feathers

Arctic tern

length = 15 inches
(380 mm)

Many birds take advantage of better conditions in different parts of the world by migrating. The commonest movements are north-south. The Arctic tern breeds in the north, migrates across the Atlantic and returns the following year.

During its life an Arctic tern may travel over 156,000 miles (250,000 km).

Altering the angle at which the wing is tilted as it pushes through the air - the angle of attack - alters how quickly or slowly the bird climbs. Too steep an angle and the wing "stalls" – air spills from beneath the wing and the bird plummets down.

Skull

Nostril

Jawbone

Beak

Vein

A **part from** mammals, birds have the largest brains, in proportion to the size of their bodies, of all animals. As in other warm-blooded animals, their high body temperature allows the brain to handle complex problems such as navigation.

Trachea

BIRD NAVIGATION AIDS

Wind

Sun

Star map

Scent

Stars

Polarized light

Magnetism

Sound

Gravity

Esophagus

Birds can navigate long distances using the position of the sun and stars, the direction of the sky's polarized light and the Earth's magnetic field.

bald eagle
length = 29 inches (725 mm)

Visual map

Birds have several different kinds of feathers that all carry out different functions. Flight feathers are long and strong. Down feathers are fluffy for warmth. They provide a covering for very young birds but are also present in adults, underneath the main feathers. Contour feathers provide the smooth outer layer of feathers that give a bird its shape. Fine, hair-like feathers called filoplumes are sensitive to touch and tell the bird when the body feathers are out of place.

Feathers are tough structures made of keratin, a substance also found in birds' beaks and the nails and claws of mammals.

The shape of its beak can tell us a lot about how a bird lives. Hummingbirds use their long beaks to reach sweet nectar from deep within flowers.

ruby-throated hummingbird

The primary feathers are the bird's main flight feathers.

The secondary feathers give the wing a large surface area.

length = 3 inches (80 mm)

Feathers must be in good condition for flight. The barbules are kept correctly hooked together by extensive preening.

Down feather

Vane

Rhachis

Rhachis

Barb

Interlocking barbules

Partly vaned feather

Calamus (quill)

Filoplumes

length = 3 inches (80 mm)

black-throated hummingbird

length = 3.5 inches (90 mm)

sicklebill hummingbird

Birds build nests to raise their young. Some are just a scrape in the soil, others are more elaborate.

Black-necked tailor birds weave a nest of leaves.

Cave swiftlets build a nest of saliva on the cave wall.

Spiders' webs, ferns and soft seeds are used for hummingbird nests.

The takahe is a large, flightless, New Zealand bird that feeds on a mixed diet using its powerful beak.

Common crossbills have a specially shaped beak for removing the seeds from pinecones.

The iiwi, found on the islands around Hawaii, has a sickle bill for feeding on nectar.

The black hornbill feeds on fruit. Its beak is also used in mating displays and for amplifying its call.

Spoonbills wade in shallow water and feed by sifting small creatures from the mud.

The delicate and long upturned bill of the black and white avocet probes mud for tiny creatures.

crossbill
length = 6.5 inches (65 mm)

iiwi
length = 5.5 inches (140 mm)

black hornbill

African spoonbill
length = 4 feet (1.3 m)

avocet

takahe

length = 25 inches (635 mm)

length = 35 inches (900 mm)

length = 17 inches (435 mm)

THE RAT

The **common rat** is the dominant rat in most of the world. It is an extremely versatile animal, living in a variety of habitats from city sewers and warehouses to farmyards. It can also live on rocky shores and in salt marshes.

RATS BELONG TO A GROUP of vertebrate animals called mammals, which are defined as being different from other vertebrates by various structural and physiological features. Mammals have a four-chambered heart, a true palate in the roof of their mouth and red blood cells without nuclei. They have a single lower jawbone that is fixed to the bony mass of the skull. They also have mammary glands that produce milk for suckling their young.

There are approximately 4,000 species of mammal, including rats, elephants, cats, shrews, bats, apes and deer. Rats are alert and intelligent animals that quickly learn to exploit new sources of food and shelter. They have adapted well to living with humans.

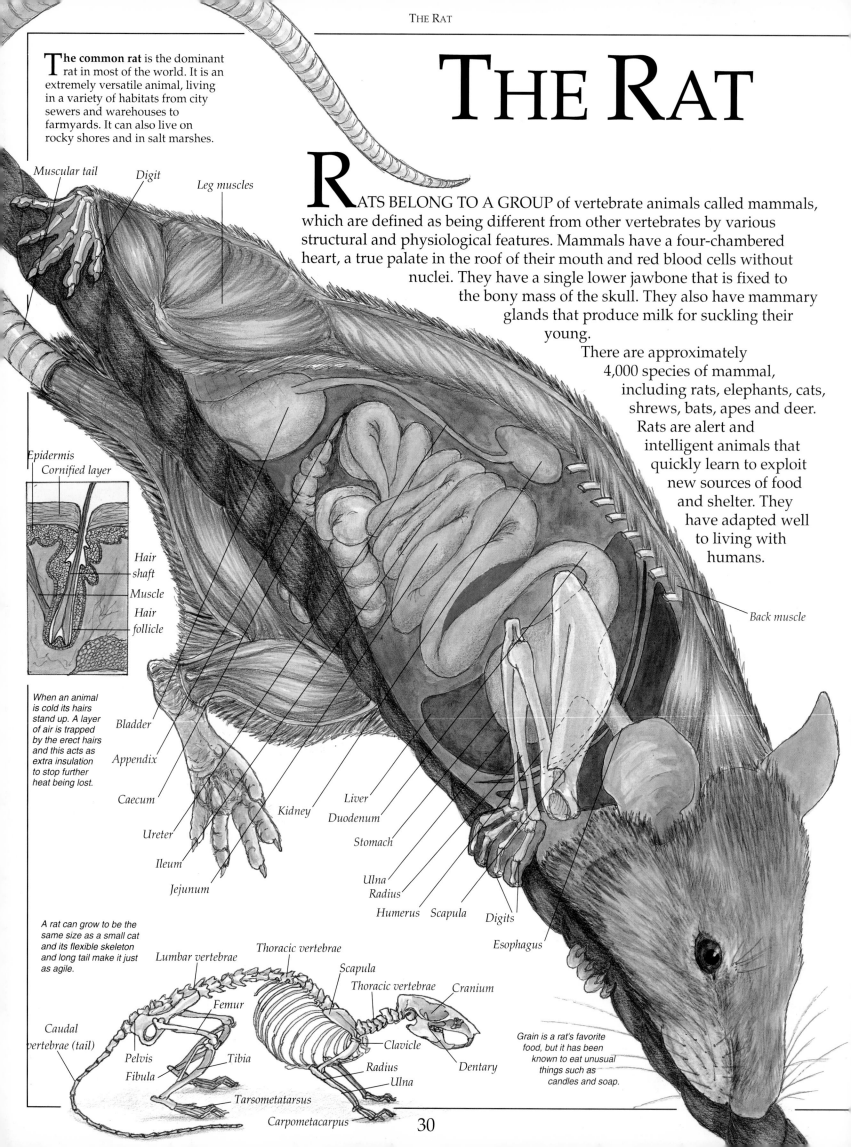

Muscular tail

Digit

Leg muscles

Epidermis

Cornified layer

Hair shaft

Muscle

Hair follicle

When an animal is cold its hairs stand up. A layer of air is trapped by the erect hairs and this acts as extra insulation to stop further heat being lost.

Bladder

Appendix

Caecum

Ureter

Ileum

Jejunum

Kidney

Liver

Duodenum

Stomach

Ulna

Radius

Humerus

Scapula

Digits

Esophagus

Back muscle

A rat can grow to be the same size as a small cat and its flexible skeleton and long tail make it just as agile.

Caudal vertebrae (tail)

Lumbar vertebrae

Thoracic vertebrae

Scapula

Thoracic vertebrae

Cranium

Femur

Clavicle

Pelvis

Tibia

Fibula

Radius

Ulna

Dentary

Tarsometatarsus

Carpometacarpus

Grain is a rat's favorite food, but it has been known to eat unusual things such as candles and soap.

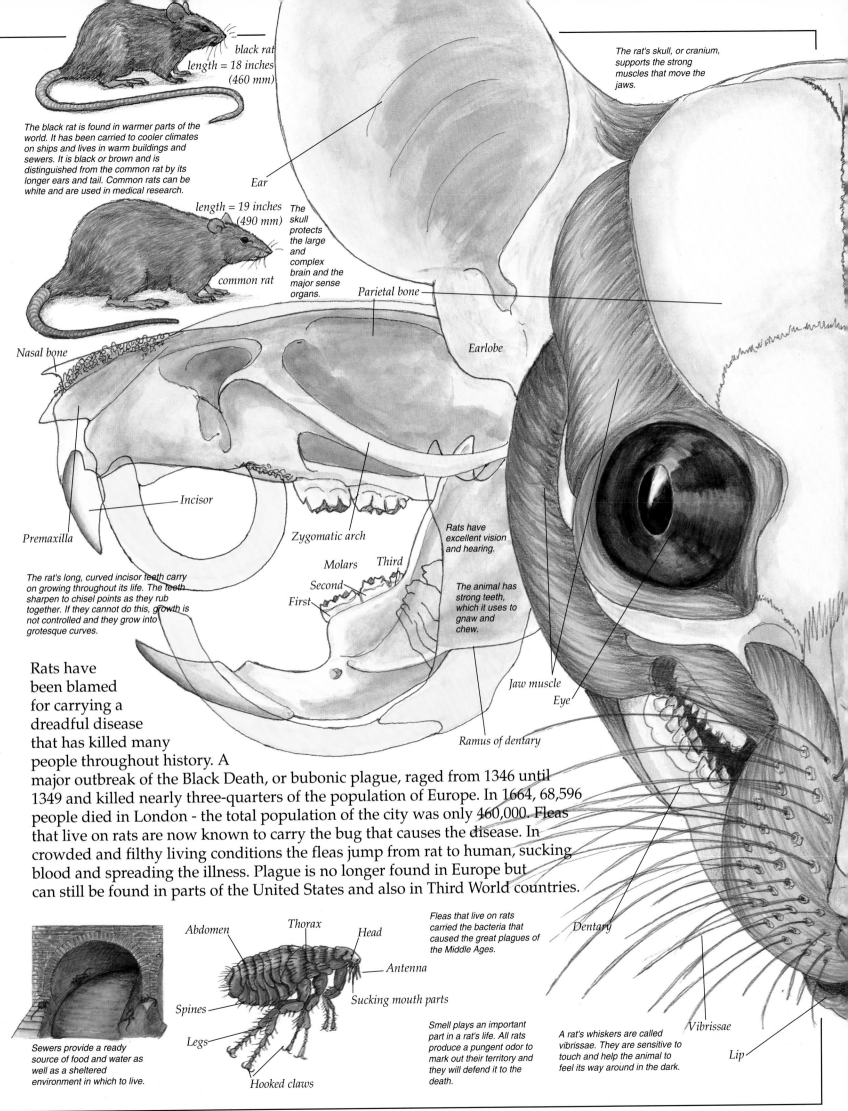

black rat
length = 18 inches
(460 mm)

The black rat is found in warmer parts of the world. It has been carried to cooler climates on ships and lives in warm buildings and sewers. It is black or brown and is distinguished from the common rat by its longer ears and tail. Common rats can be white and are used in medical research.

length = 19 inches
(490 mm)

common rat

The rat's skull, or cranium, supports the strong muscles that move the jaws.

Ear

The skull protects the large and complex brain and the major sense organs.

Parietal bone

Earlobe

Nasal bone

Incisor

Premaxilla

Zygomatic arch

Molars Third
Second
First

Rats have excellent vision and hearing.

The animal has strong teeth, which it uses to gnaw and chew.

The rat's long, curved incisor teeth carry on growing throughout its life. The teeth sharpen to chisel points as they rub together. If they cannot do this, growth is not controlled and they grow into grotesque curves.

Jaw muscle
Eye

Ramus of dentary

Rats have been blamed for carrying a dreadful disease that has killed many people throughout history. A major outbreak of the Black Death, or bubonic plague, raged from 1346 until 1349 and killed nearly three-quarters of the population of Europe. In 1664, 68,596 people died in London - the total population of the city was only 460,000. Fleas that live on rats are now known to carry the bug that causes the disease. In crowded and filthy living conditions the fleas jump from rat to human, sucking blood and spreading the illness. Plague is no longer found in Europe but can still be found in parts of the United States and also in Third World countries.

Abdomen   Thorax   Head

Fleas that live on rats carried the bacteria that caused the great plagues of the Middle Ages.

Dentary

Antenna

Spines

Sucking mouth parts

Legs

Sewers provide a ready source of food and water as well as a sheltered environment in which to live.

Hooked claws

Smell plays an important part in a rat's life. All rats produce a pungent odor to mark out their territory and they will defend it to the death.

A rat's whiskers are called vibrissae. They are sensitive to touch and help the animal to feel its way around in the dark.

Vibrissae

Lip

THE RAT AND OTHER
RODENTS

RATS BELONG TO A GROUP WITHIN THE MAMMALS called rodents, which all have the same type of skull and teeth. The powerful muscles of their jaws and the teeth that are designed for gnawing give rodents their blunt, rounded face and head. The group includes rats and mice, dormice, gerbils, beavers, squirrels, porcupines, chinchillas, pacas, voles, hamsters and chipmunks.

With their sharp chisel-like incisors, rodents can eat grass, roots, tubers and wood - they can even cut down trees. Black rats crave water and have been known to gnaw through lead pipes to get at the water inside. Other rodents have cheek pouches that open near the corners of the mouth and are used to carry food back to the nest.

Rodents are found all over the world, from the Arctic to the tropical forests. They are diverse in form and are adaptable and resourceful and can live in a variety of different environments. Generally they exist in abundance in most land areas and have a high birthrate. A pair of rats can produce 16 litters per year. As each litter has an average of ten young, in their lifetime of five years a breeding couple can produce 800 new rats. Rapid breeding permits them to maintain a stable population despite predators, many of which rely on rats as their main source of food.

Small rodents can be difficult to see. Many come out only at night, and those that come out in the day usually stay well hidden in dense undergrowth.

Flattened tail

Muscles of tail

Muscles of hind-leg

Petagium

Flying squirrels make nests of twigs and leaves in hollow tree trunks and branches. Large skin flaps stretched between their front and back legs enable them to glide between trees. A rod of cartilage extends from the outer edge of their wrist and acts as a spreader. Flying squirrels are extremely agile and, if they slip and fall, are seldom hurt. A Mexican flying squirrel once leapt down a precipice to land unharmed on a ledge 600 feet (180 m) below. A more usual glide may just reach 220 feet (65 m). Their flattened tail acts as a rudder, an airbrake and as a cloak to wrap up the resting animal.

Mole rats live permanently underground in an extensive maze of burrows. Because they do not rely on sight to survive, their eyes have become weak and they are almost blind. In order to navigate their burrows they have developed a method of echolocation, using sound to find their way about.

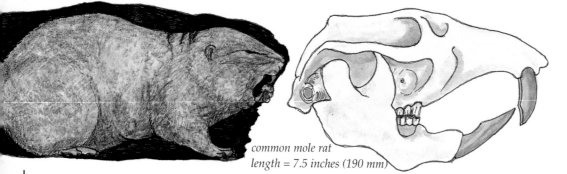

common mole rat
length = 7.5 inches (190 mm)

Beavers, one of the largest rodents, have a massive skull. Their incisors are well developed and are ideal for cutting and felling trees.

The enormous, flat and scaly tail of the beaver makes it a good swimmer. Its dense water-proof fur keeps it warm and dry in cold winters.

Mole rats have short legs and a powerful body. They recognize unknown objects by touching them with their sensitive nose.

The mole rat's strong skull has projecting incisors to dig tunnels. It has strong clawed feet for scraping soil out of the burrow as it digs.

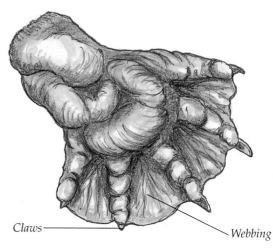

Claws

Webbing

beaver
length = 4.6 feet (1.4 m)

Skull

Molar

Lower jaw

Incisor

Webbed toes on its back legs push a beaver through the water as it swims. Fingers on the forepaws can grip the young hardwood branches used for building and for food.

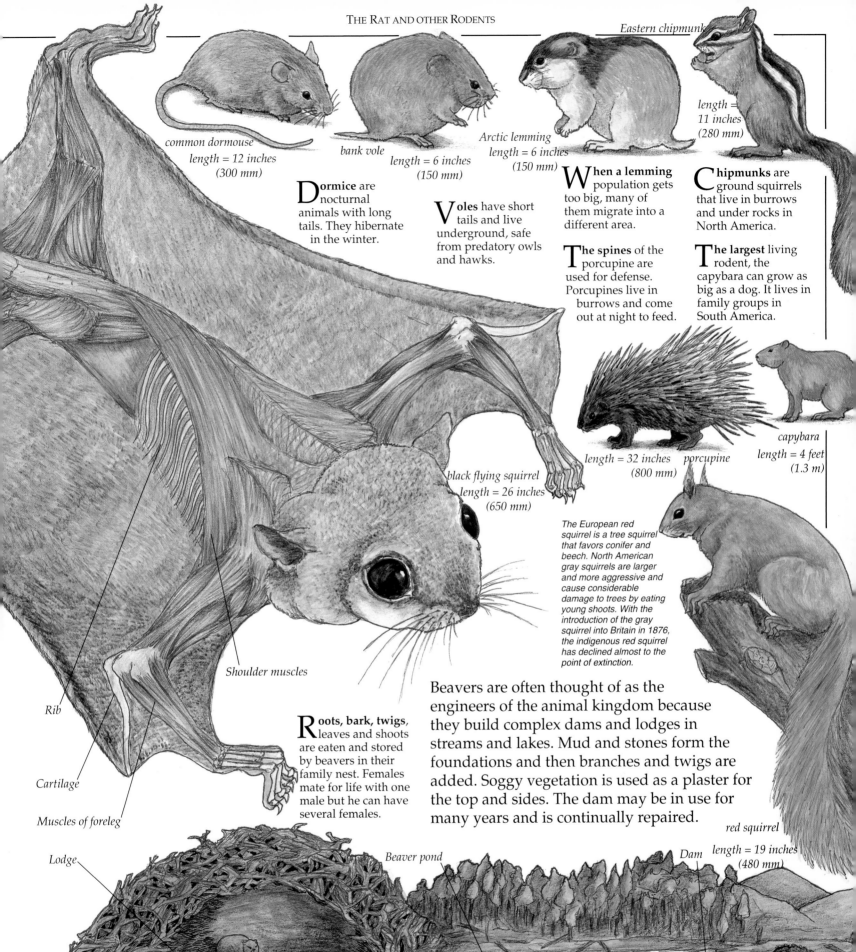

Eastern chipmunk

common dormouse
length = 12 inches
(300 mm)

bank vole
length = 6 inches
(150 mm)

Arctic lemming
length = 6 inches
(150 mm)

length = 11 inches (280 mm)

Dormice are nocturnal animals with long tails. They hibernate in the winter.

Voles have short tails and live underground, safe from predatory owls and hawks.

When a lemming population gets too big, many of them migrate into a different area.

Chipmunks are ground squirrels that live in burrows and under rocks in North America.

The spines of the porcupine are used for defense. Porcupines live in burrows and come out at night to feed.

The largest living rodent, the capybara can grow as big as a dog. It lives in family groups in South America.

length = 32 inches (800 mm) *porcupine*

capybara length = 4 feet (1.3 m)

black flying squirrel length = 26 inches (650 mm)

The European red squirrel is a tree squirrel that favors conifer and beech. North American gray squirrels are larger and more aggressive and cause considerable damage to trees by eating young shoots. With the introduction of the gray squirrel into Britain in 1876, the indigenous red squirrel has declined almost to the point of extinction.

Shoulder muscles

Rib

Cartilage

Muscles of foreleg

Roots, bark, twigs, leaves and shoots are eaten and stored by beavers in their family nest. Females mate for life with one male but he can have several females.

Beavers are often thought of as the engineers of the animal kingdom because they build complex dams and lodges in streams and lakes. Mud and stones form the foundations and then branches and twigs are added. Soggy vegetation is used as a plaster for the top and sides. The dam may be in use for many years and is continually repaired.

red squirrel

Lodge

Beaver pond

Dam

length = 19 inches (480 mm)

The entrance to the beavers' nest, or lodge, is under the water level and is usually positioned close to the dam.

THE TIGER

Tigers are carnivores - mammals that eat meat. They are found throughout India, southern China, the Malay peninsula, Sumatra, Java and Bali. Lions, jaguars, leopards and panthers are all close relatives of tigers. These are collectively known as the big cats.

From the tip of the nose to the end of the tail a tiger can measure 12 feet (3.5 m). Its striped coat helps to break up the outline of its body, allowing it to blend in with the surrounding vegetation so that it can stalk its prey without being seen. The pale-colored Siberian tiger is found in the cold forests of Manchuria and Siberia.

Nearly all cats have patterned fur for the purpose of camouflage but there is a disadvantage: the skins of many large cats have been sought as hunting trophies or have been used to supply people with fur coats. Big cats have also been hunted to prevent them eating livestock. Hunting has forced some cats to the verge of extinction.

The teeth of the tiger are perfect tools for devouring big animals such as deer and cattle. Dagger-like fangs, the canines, tear the prey open. Chisel-like incisors rip through the tough skin to reach the flesh below and nibble the meat from bones. Razor-sharp molars, the carnassials, slice through flesh, like scissors through cloth.

canine tooth

crest

carnassial tooth *mandible*

premolar tooth

Powerful muscles slam the strong jaws, with their sharp teeth, together, cutting skin, flesh and bone. Long jaws would be weak and incapable of biting so hard, so all carnivores have much shorter jaws and flatter faces than herbivores.

lip and face muscles

main jaw muscle

masseter muscle

chest muscles

skin

tiger
length = 7.5 inches (190 mm)

Large eyes, a keen sense of smell and acute hearing all go to make an efficient predator.

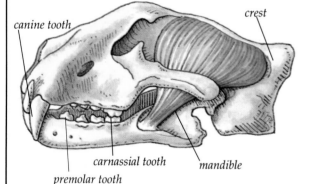

muscle

tendons

extended claw

Broad, sensitive, pad-like feet let the tiger creep silently through the forest to get close to its prey.

Knife-like claws grip the tiger's victim and tear it open, cutting blood vessels. The claws are tucked away unless needed and are used for climbing.

weasel
length = 11 inches (280 mm)

Slender, lithe and short-legged, weasels and their relatives are vicious nocturnal predators.

Egyptian mongoose
length = 3.6 feet (1.1 m)

Some mongooses kill cobras and other venomous snakes. They are not immune to the venom but avoid snakebites.

striped skunk
length = 25 inches (620 mm)

The skunk's markings warn predators that it does not make a pleasant meal. It can spray a foul-smelling fluid.

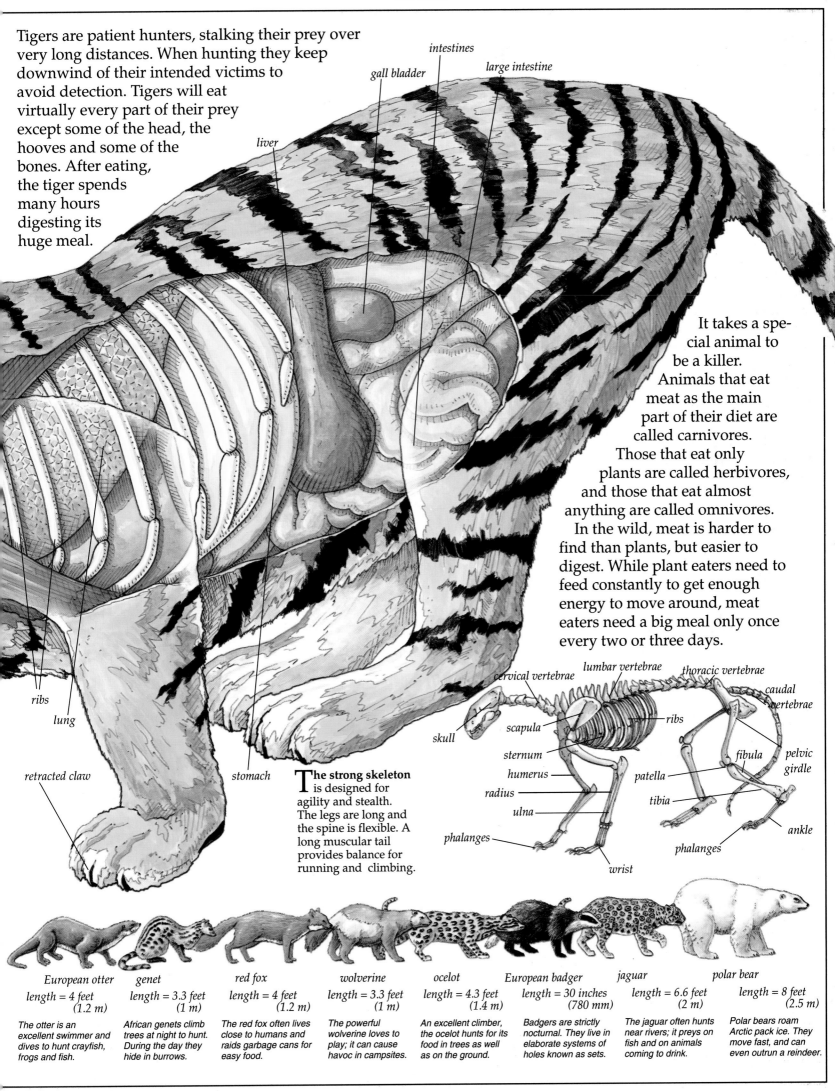

Tigers are patient hunters, stalking their prey over very long distances. When hunting they keep downwind of their intended victims to avoid detection. Tigers will eat virtually every part of their prey except some of the head, the hooves and some of the bones. After eating, the tiger spends many hours digesting its huge meal.

intestines

large intestine

gall bladder

liver

ribs

lung

retracted claw

stomach

It takes a special animal to be a killer. Animals that eat meat as the main part of their diet are called carnivores. Those that eat only plants are called herbivores, and those that eat almost anything are called omnivores. In the wild, meat is harder to find than plants, but easier to digest. While plant eaters need to feed constantly to get enough energy to move around, meat eaters need a big meal only once every two or three days.

The strong skeleton is designed for agility and stealth. The legs are long and the spine is flexible. A long muscular tail provides balance for running and climbing.

cervical vertebrae

lumbar vertebrae

thoracic vertebrae

caudal vertebrae

skull

scapula

ribs

sternum

humerus

patella

fibula

pelvic girdle

radius

tibia

ulna

ankle

phalanges

phalanges

wrist

European otter
length = 4 feet
(1.2 m)

The otter is an excellent swimmer and dives to hunt crayfish, frogs and fish.

genet
length = 3.3 feet
(1 m)

African genets climb trees at night to hunt. During the day they hide in burrows.

red fox
length = 4 feet
(1.2 m)

The red fox often lives close to humans and raids garbage cans for easy food.

wolverine
length = 3.3 feet
(1 m)

The powerful wolverine loves to play; it can cause havoc in campsites.

ocelot
length = 4.3 feet
(1.4 m)

An excellent climber, the ocelot hunts for its food in trees as well as on the ground.

European badger
length = 30 inches
(780 mm)

Badgers are strictly nocturnal. They live in elaborate systems of holes known as sets.

jaguar
length = 6.6 feet
(2 m)

The jaguar often hunts near rivers; it preys on fish and on animals coming to drink.

polar bear
length = 8 feet
(2.5 m)

Polar bears roam Arctic pack ice. They move fast, and can even outrun a reindeer.

*cheetah   length = 7 feet
(2.2 m)*

THE TIGER AND OTHER
BIG CATS

BIG CATS ARE CARNIVORES: they are meat eaters. Other carnivorous mammals include the small cats, dogs, foxes, wolves, hyenas, bears, pandas, raccoons, weasels, stoats, badgers, skunks, otters, mongooses and civets. They range in size from the weasel which is 11 inches (280 mm) long and weighs 2.5 ounces (70 g), to the big brown bear of Alaska, which has a height of 10 feet (3 m) and a weight of over 350 pounds (780 kg).

To catch their prey cheetahs stalk it, and then race to catch it, sometimes as far as 610 yards (550 m).

Lithe and slim with long legs and powerful leg muscles, cheetahs are high-speed chasers.

Cheetahs are able to reach speeds of over 69 miles (110 km) per hour during a high-speed chase.

*spotted hyena
length = 4 feet (1.3 m)*

A short, flattened face enables a big cat to deliver a powerful bite. Strong muscles are attached to a large crest on top of the head, and these close the jaws. Forward-facing eyes provide binocular vision, essential for an animal that hunts.

Hyenas are very efficient predators: they have the most powerful jaws of all the carnivores, and are quite capable of biting through the leg of a man in one go. Their muscular head, powerful shoulders and habit of hunting in packs over large areas make hyenas formidable predators. Spotted hyenas can be extremely ferocious and have been known to kill an old lion, and even a half-grown rhinoceros. Sometimes a persistent pack of hyenas will even force a pride of lions to abandon their kill.

*extinct smilodon
length = 10 feet (3 m)*

*leopard
length = 7 feet
(2.2 m)*

Many species of big cats that roamed the earth thousands of years ago are now extinct. In Europe, *Homotherium*, a large scimitar-toothed cat, was common. It could have killed an animal as big as a young elephant.

The lion's long, mobile tail has a small tuft of dark hairs at its tip. Young cubs often play with the adult's tail tuft, to practice the pouncing movement used in hunting.

The big cats use scent, in the form of pungent urine, glandular secretions and feces, to mark out their territory.

Many big cats rub against the scent they have applied. This identifies the individual making the scent mark.

The sense of smell is well developed in carnivores. They use it to help them hunt, follow trails and detect enemies.

Cubs are not competent hunters until they are eighteen months old and so depend on older cats for food.

*lion
length = 7 feet (2.2 m)*

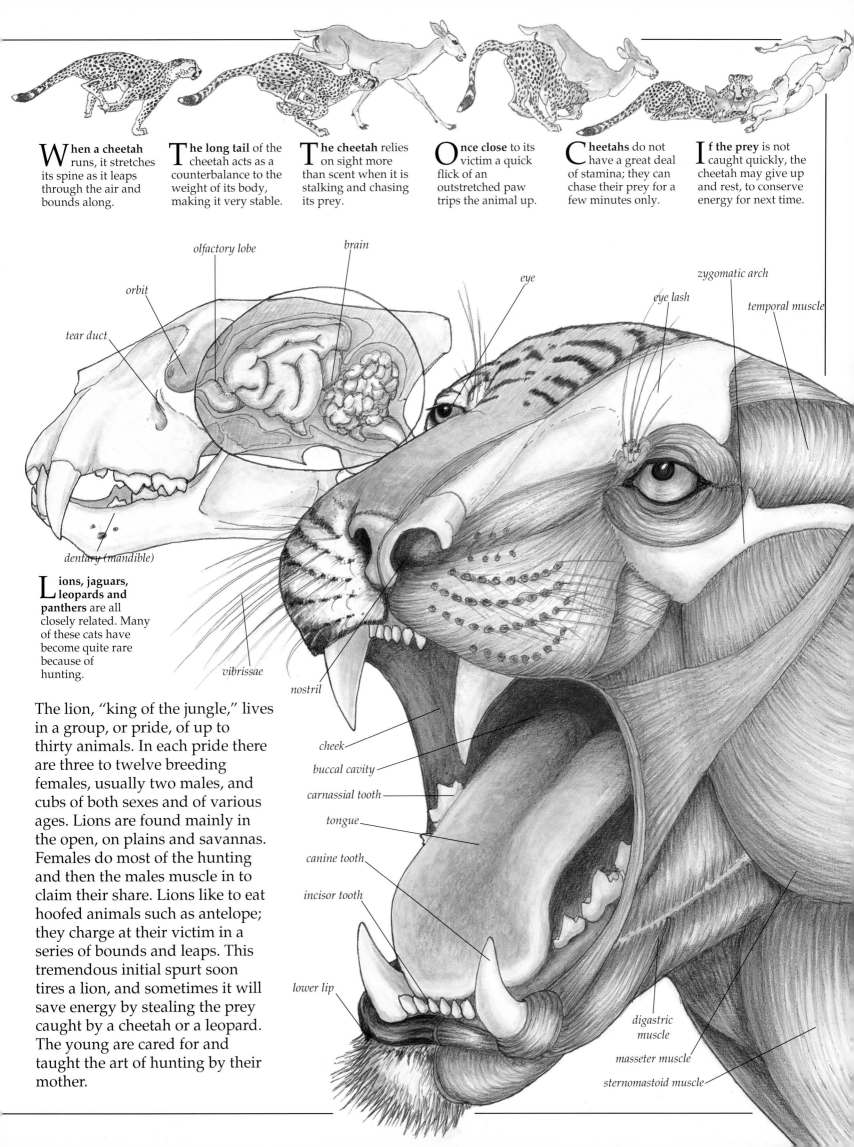

When a cheetah runs, it stretches its spine as it leaps through the air and bounds along.

The long tail of the cheetah acts as a counterbalance to the weight of its body, making it very stable.

The cheetah relies on sight more than scent when it is stalking and chasing its prey.

Once close to its victim a quick flick of an outstretched paw trips the animal up.

Cheetahs do not have a great deal of stamina; they can chase their prey for a few minutes only.

If the prey is not caught quickly, the cheetah may give up and rest, to conserve energy for next time.

olfactory lobe

brain

orbit

tear duct

eye

zygomatic arch

eye lash

temporal muscle

dentary (mandible)

Lions, jaguars, leopards and **panthers** are all closely related. Many of these cats have become quite rare because of hunting.

vibrissae

nostril

cheek

buccal cavity

carnassial tooth

tongue

canine tooth

incisor tooth

lower lip

digastric muscle

masseter muscle

sternomastoid muscle

The lion, "king of the jungle," lives in a group, or pride, of up to thirty animals. In each pride there are three to twelve breeding females, usually two males, and cubs of both sexes and of various ages. Lions are found mainly in the open, on plains and savannas. Females do most of the hunting and then the males muscle in to claim their share. Lions like to eat hoofed animals such as antelope; they charge at their victim in a series of bounds and leaps. This tremendous initial spurt soon tires a lion, and sometimes it will save energy by stealing the prey caught by a cheetah or a leopard. The young are cared for and taught the art of hunting by their mother.

THE ELEPHANT

Brain *Hollow skull* *Thick skin*

The elephant's huge ears act as radiators, with fine blood vessels just below the surface of the skin. These lose heat easily and prevent overheating.

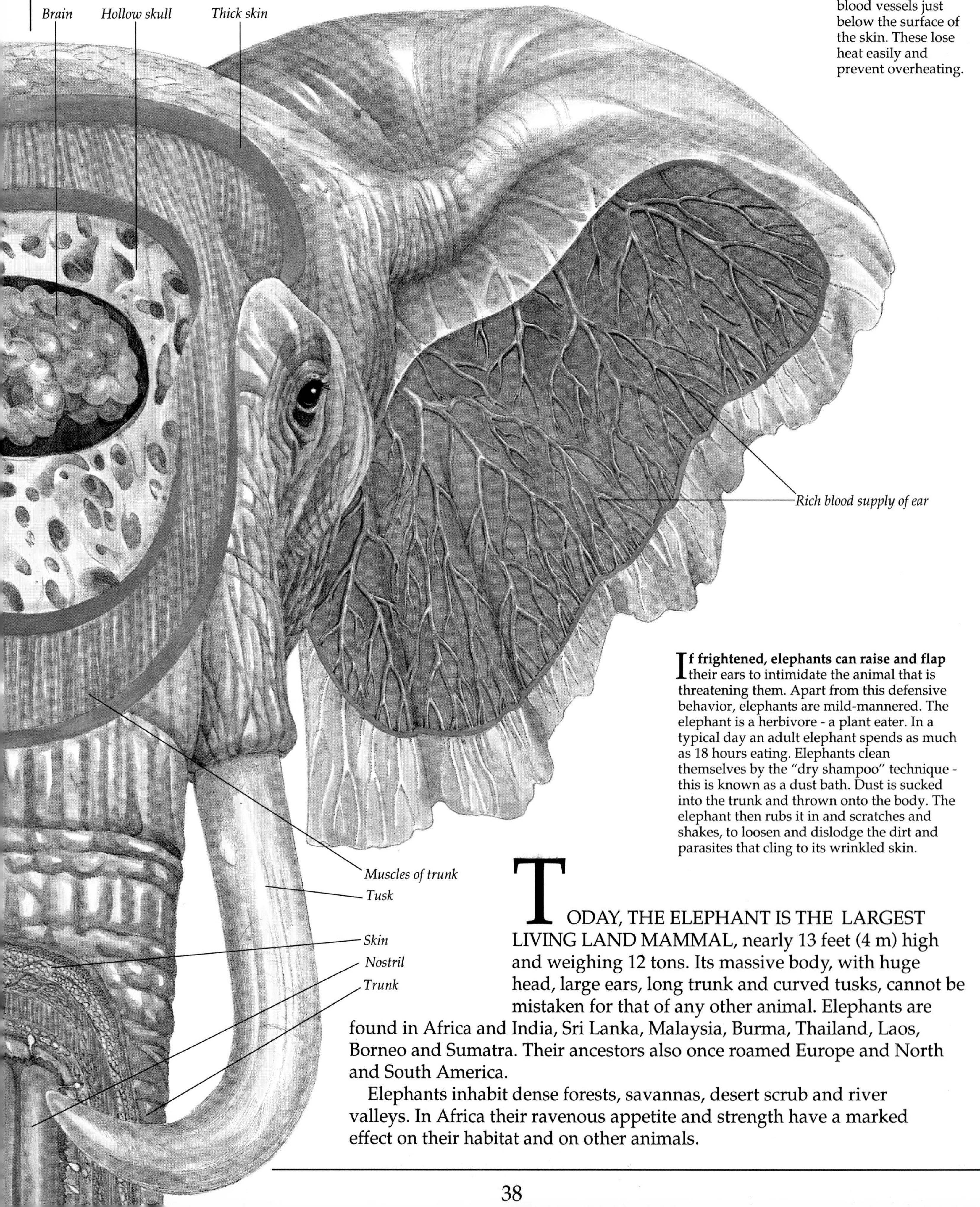

Rich blood supply of ear

Muscles of trunk
Tusk

Skin
Nostril
Trunk

If frightened, elephants can raise and flap their ears to intimidate the animal that is threatening them. Apart from this defensive behavior, elephants are mild-mannered. The elephant is a herbivore - a plant eater. In a typical day an adult elephant spends as much as 18 hours eating. Elephants clean themselves by the "dry shampoo" technique - this is known as a dust bath. Dust is sucked into the trunk and thrown onto the body. The elephant then rubs it in and scratches and shakes, to loosen and dislodge the dirt and parasites that cling to its wrinkled skin.

TODAY, THE ELEPHANT IS THE LARGEST LIVING LAND MAMMAL, nearly 13 feet (4 m) high and weighing 12 tons. Its massive body, with huge head, large ears, long trunk and curved tusks, cannot be mistaken for that of any other animal. Elephants are found in Africa and India, Sri Lanka, Malaysia, Burma, Thailand, Laos, Borneo and Sumatra. Their ancestors also once roamed Europe and North and South America.

Elephants inhabit dense forests, savannas, desert scrub and river valleys. In Africa their ravenous appetite and strength have a marked effect on their habitat and on other animals.

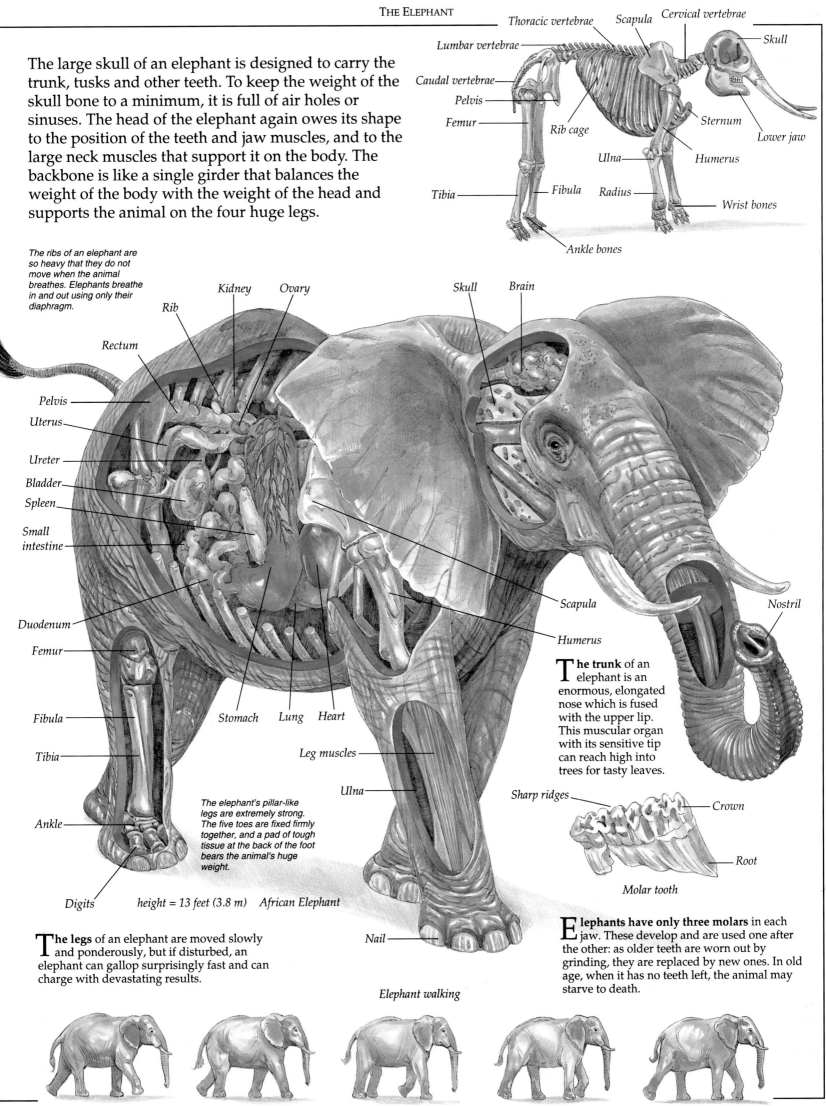

The large skull of an elephant is designed to carry the trunk, tusks and other teeth. To keep the weight of the skull bone to a minimum, it is full of air holes or sinuses. The head of the elephant again owes its shape to the position of the teeth and jaw muscles, and to the large neck muscles that support it on the body. The backbone is like a single girder that balances the weight of the body with the weight of the head and supports the animal on the four huge legs.

Thoracic vertebrae
Scapula
Cervical vertebrae
Lumbar vertebrae
Skull
Caudal vertebrae
Pelvis
Femur
Rib cage
Sternum
Lower jaw
Ulna
Humerus
Tibia
Fibula
Radius
Wrist bones
Ankle bones

The ribs of an elephant are so heavy that they do not move when the animal breathes. Elephants breathe in and out using only their diaphragm.

Kidney
Ovary
Skull
Brain
Rib
Rectum
Pelvis
Uterus
Ureter
Bladder
Spleen
Small intestine
Scapula
Duodenum
Humerus
Femur
Fibula
Tibia
Stomach
Lung
Heart
Leg muscles
Ankle
Ulna
Digits
Nail

The elephant's pillar-like legs are extremely strong. The five toes are fixed firmly together, and a pad of tough tissue at the back of the foot bears the animal's huge weight.

height = 13 feet (3.8 m)   African Elephant

Nostril

The trunk of an elephant is an enormous, elongated nose which is fused with the upper lip. This muscular organ with its sensitive tip can reach high into trees for tasty leaves.

Sharp ridges
Crown
Root
Molar tooth

The legs of an elephant are moved slowly and ponderously, but if disturbed, an elephant can gallop surprisingly fast and can charge with devastating results.

Elephants have only three molars in each jaw. These develop and are used one after the other: as older teeth are worn out by grinding, they are replaced by new ones. In old age, when it has no teeth left, the animal may starve to death.

Elephant walking

The Elephant and other Large Mammals

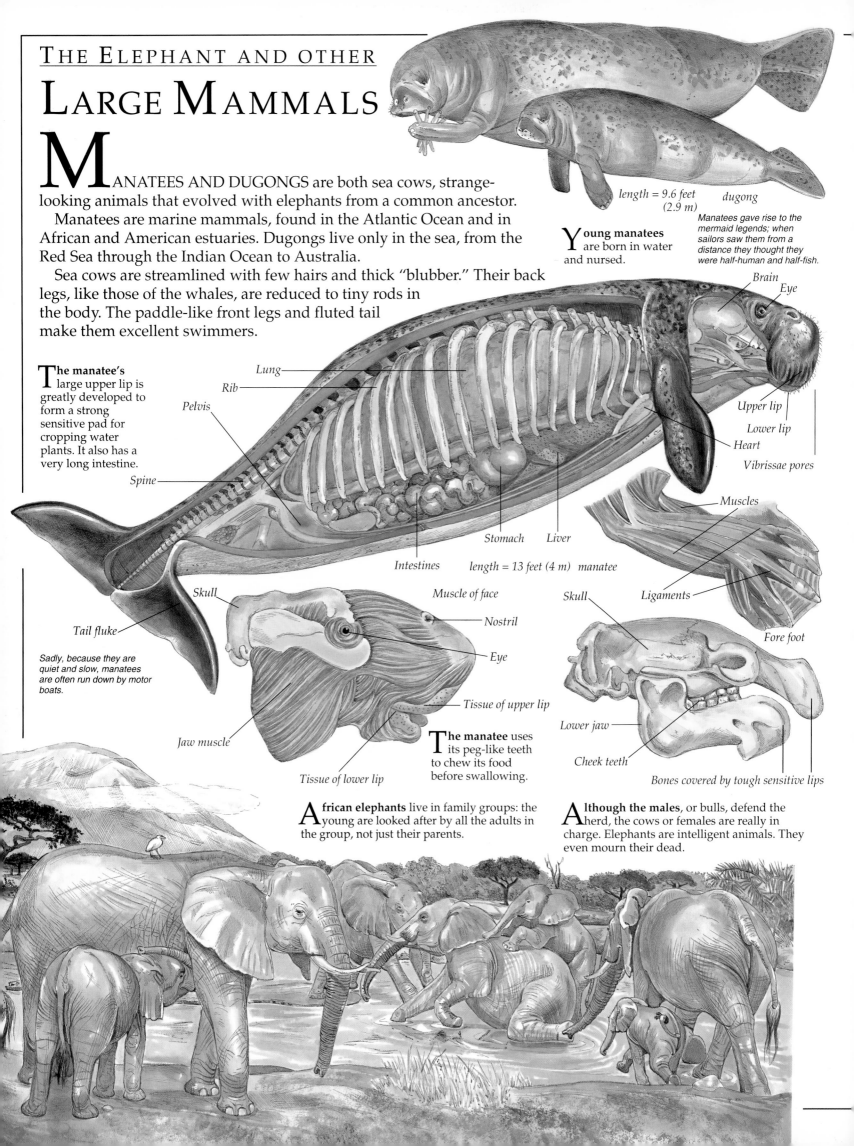

MANATEES AND DUGONGS are both sea cows, strange-looking animals that evolved with elephants from a common ancestor.

Manatees are marine mammals, found in the Atlantic Ocean and in African and American estuaries. Dugongs live only in the sea, from the Red Sea through the Indian Ocean to Australia.

Sea cows are streamlined with few hairs and thick "blubber." Their back legs, like those of the whales, are reduced to tiny rods in the body. The paddle-like front legs and fluted tail make them excellent swimmers.

length = 9.6 feet (2.9 m)   *dugong*

Young manatees are born in water and nursed.

Manatees gave rise to the mermaid legends; when sailors saw them from a distance they thought they were half-human and half-fish.

The manatee's large upper lip is greatly developed to form a strong sensitive pad for cropping water plants. It also has a very long intestine.

Brain
Eye
Upper lip
Lower lip
Heart
Vibrissae pores
Lung
Rib
Pelvis
Spine
Stomach
Liver
Intestines
length = 13 feet (4 m) manatee
Muscles
Ligaments
Fore foot

Skull
Tail fluke

Sadly, because they are quiet and slow, manatees are often run down by motor boats.

Muscle of face
Nostril
Eye
Skull
Lower jaw
Cheek teeth
Tissue of upper lip
Jaw muscle
Tissue of lower lip

The manatee uses its peg-like teeth to chew its food before swallowing.

Bones covered by tough sensitive lips

African elephants live in family groups: the young are looked after by all the adults in the group, not just their parents.

Although the males, or bulls, defend the herd, the cows or females are really in charge. Elephants are intelligent animals. They even mourn their dead.

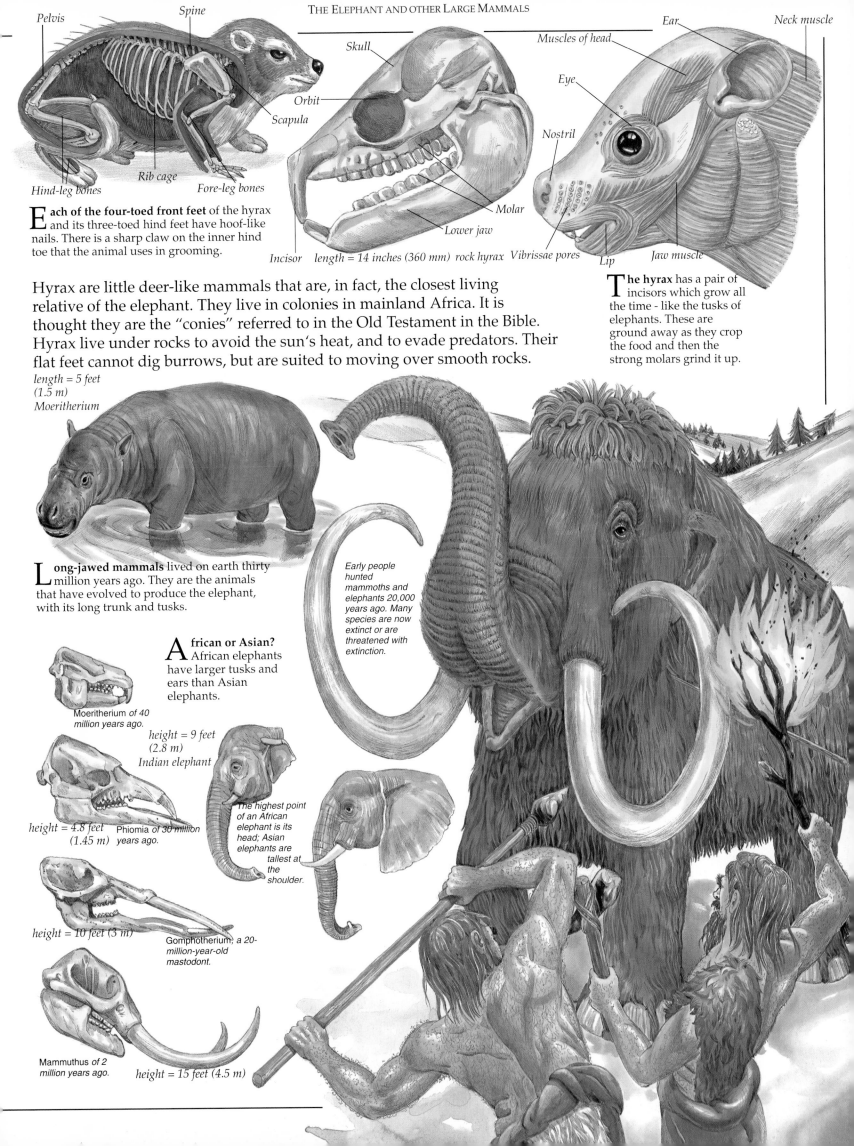

Pelvis

Spine

Skull

Muscles of head

Ear

Neck muscle

Orbit

Eye

Scapula

Nostril

Hind-leg bones

Rib cage

Fore-leg bones

Molar

Lower jaw

Incisor

Vibrissae pores

Lip

Jaw muscle

length = 14 inches (360 mm) rock hyrax

Each of the four-toed front feet of the hyrax and its three-toed hind feet have hoof-like nails. There is a sharp claw on the inner hind toe that the animal uses in grooming.

The hyrax has a pair of incisors which grow all the time - like the tusks of elephants. These are ground away as they crop the food and then the strong molars grind it up.

Hyrax are little deer-like mammals that are, in fact, the closest living relative of the elephant. They live in colonies in mainland Africa. It is thought they are the "conies" referred to in the Old Testament in the Bible. Hyrax live under rocks to avoid the sun's heat, and to evade predators. Their flat feet cannot dig burrows, but are suited to moving over smooth rocks.

length = 5 feet (1.5 m) Moeritherium

Long-jawed mammals lived on earth thirty million years ago. They are the animals that have evolved to produce the elephant, with its long trunk and tusks.

Early people hunted mammoths and elephants 20,000 years ago. Many species are now extinct or are threatened with extinction.

African or Asian? African elephants have larger tusks and ears than Asian elephants.

Moeritherium of 40 million years ago.

height = 9 feet (2.8 m) Indian elephant

height = 4.8 feet (1.45 m) Phiomia of 30 million years ago.

The highest point of an African elephant is its head; Asian elephants are tallest at the shoulder.

height = 10 feet (3 m)

Gomphotherium, a 20-million-year-old mastodont.

Mammuthus of 2 million years ago.

height = 15 feet (4.5 m)

THE WHALE

length = 5.5 feet (16.5 m) right whale

Callosity

Upper jaw

WHALES ARE MAMMALS - a fact that you may find surprising, as they spend their whole lives in the sea. Whales, along with dolphins and porpoises, are known as cetaceans. The earliest cetaceans appeared some 50 million years ago, and were quite small land animals, with four small legs. They have become very much modified from their early ancestors and are now adapted to life in the water.

Flippers are all that remain of the front legs. Each flipper has bones equivalent to those of the human hand and arm. These guide and steer the animals as they swim. Back legs are not visible - but the remains of these legs can be found as tiny bones hidden beneath the skin in the body.

A powerful muscular tail with broad flukes propels the whale through the water. Some cetaceans, including dolphins and killer whales, are very fast swimmers. The large dorsal fin keeps the animal upright as it swims and prevents rolling.

Baleen

Tongue

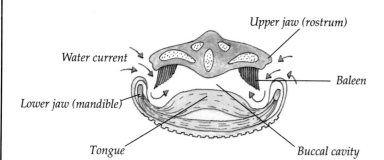

Upper jaw (rostrum)

Water current

Baleen

Lower jaw (mandible)

Tongue

Buccal cavity

All mammals are warm-blooded, and most land species have a furry coat. In water fur would slow the whale down so, to keep warm, it has a layer of fatty tissue, called blubber, under the skin. In some whales this is 20 inches (50 cm) thick. Processed blubber, or "whale oil," was once used for making soap and margarine, and was burned to provide lighting on ships.

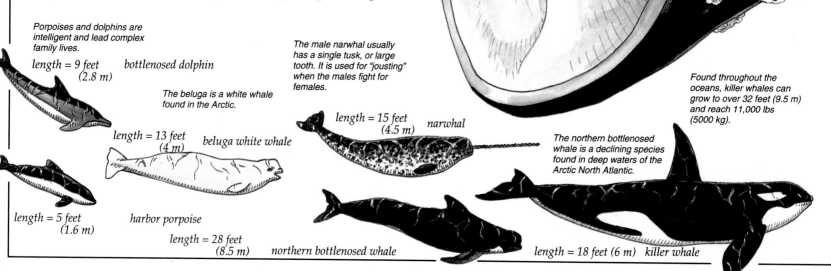

Porpoises and dolphins are intelligent and lead complex family lives.

length = 9 feet (2.8 m)   bottlenosed dolphin

The beluga is a white whale found in the Arctic.

The male narwhal usually has a single tusk, or large tooth. It is used for "jousting" when the males fight for females.

length = 13 feet (4 m)   beluga white whale

length = 15 feet (4.5 m) narwhal

Found throughout the oceans, killer whales can grow to over 32 feet (9.5 m) and reach 11,000 lbs (5000 kg).

The northern bottlenosed whale is a declining species found in deep waters of the Arctic North Atlantic.

length = 5 feet (1.6 m)   harbor porpoise

length = 28 feet (8.5 m)   northern bottlenosed whale

length = 18 feet (6 m) killer whale

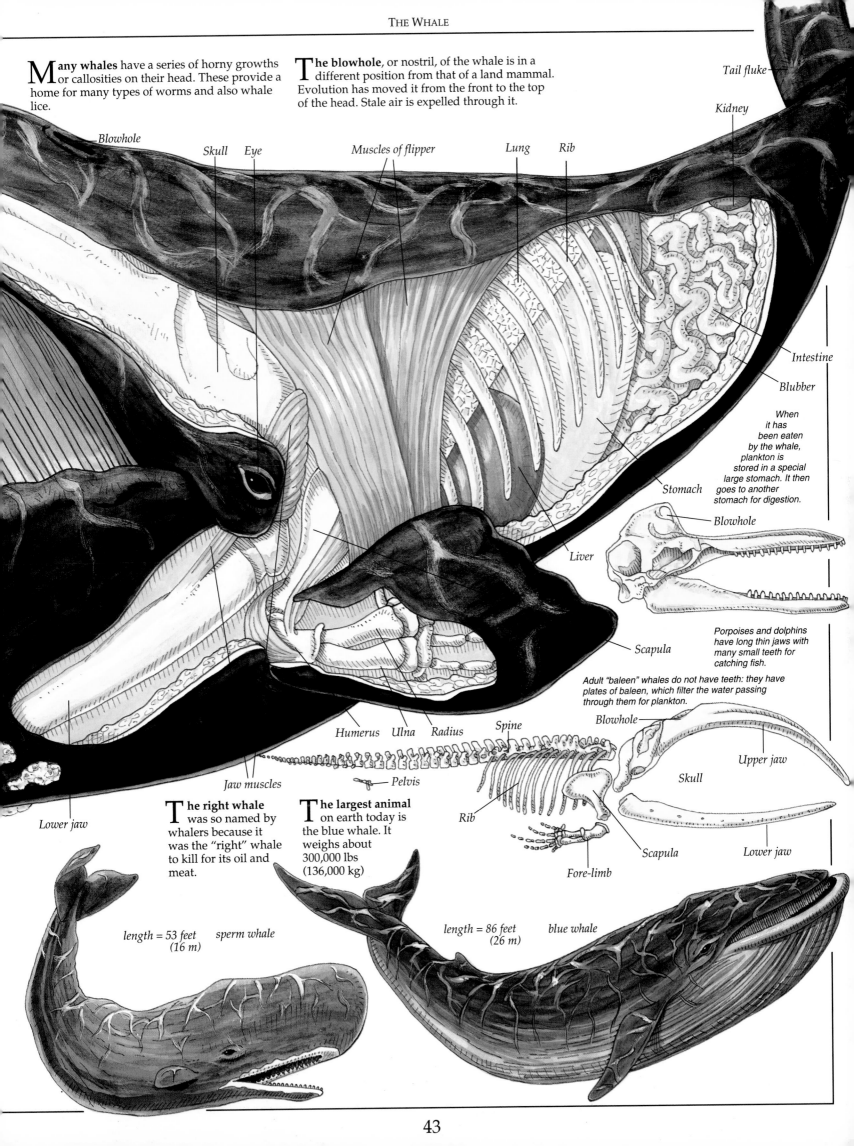

Many whales have a series of horny growths or callosities on their head. These provide a home for many types of worms and also whale lice.

The blowhole, or nostril, of the whale is in a different position from that of a land mammal. Evolution has moved it from the front to the top of the head. Stale air is expelled through it.

Tail fluke

Kidney

Blowhole

Skull   Eye   Muscles of flipper   Lung   Rib

Intestine

Blubber

When it has been eaten by the whale, plankton is stored in a special large stomach. It then goes to another stomach for digestion.

Stomach

Blowhole

Liver

Scapula

Porpoises and dolphins have long thin jaws with many small teeth for catching fish.

Adult "baleen" whales do not have teeth: they have plates of baleen, which filter the water passing through them for plankton.

Blowhole

Upper jaw

Skull

Spine

Rib

Scapula

Lower jaw

Fore-limb

Humerus   Ulna   Radius

Pelvis

Jaw muscles

Lower jaw

The right whale was so named by whalers because it was the "right" whale to kill for its oil and meat.

The largest animal on earth today is the blue whale. It weighs about 300,000 lbs (136,000 kg)

length = 53 feet (16 m)   sperm whale

length = 86 feet (26 m)   blue whale

THE WHALE AND OTHER
SEA MAMMALS

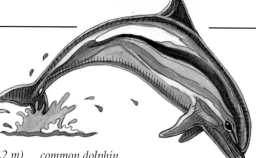

length = 7 feet (2.2 m)   common dolphin

W HALES SPEND A LOT OF THEIR TIME
below the sea surface. Some whales can stay under
water for up to an hour. Whales are specially
adapted for diving. They do not breathe underwater, and although the
blood supply continues to the brain and heart, it is reduced to other parts
of the body, and the heartbeat slows during a dive. The sperm whale is
recorded as performing the deepest dive; it went down to 10,000 feet
(3,000 m). Baleen whales do not dive very deeply since most of their food
is found in the upper layers of the sea.

Dolphins often leap from the water as they cruise along at about
10.2 miles (17 km) per hour and they can swim over enormous distances.

Nostril

Muscle

Eye

Skull

Upper lip

Vibrissae

Mandible

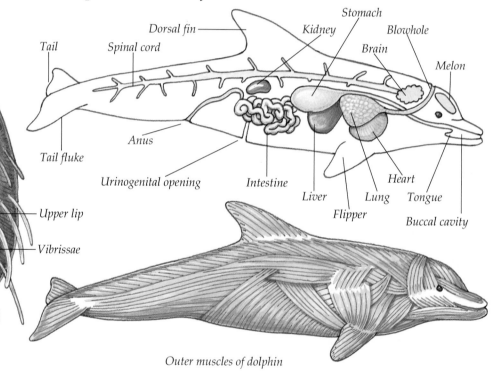

Tail

Spinal cord

Dorsal fin

Tail fluke

Anus

Urinogenital opening

Intestine

Liver

Flipper

Lung

Kidney

Stomach

Brain

Blowhole

Melon

Heart

Tongue

Buccal cavity

Outer muscles of dolphin

Seals, sealions and walruses are also marine mammals, and are all
carnivores. Unlike whales, they still have legs that have webbed fingers
and toes for swimming. They can swim fast and can reach speeds of 22
miles (35 km) per hour. Their strong neck vertebrae are fixed to a very
flexible backbone, which lets them make sharp turns when swimming.
Humans have found that, in captivity, these animals are capable of clever
balancing tricks on land.

The walrus is
found in southern
latitudes. It has
enormous tusks and
dagger-like incisor
teeth, which it uses
for digging up
shellfish. Bull
walruses use the
tusks when fighting
each other over the
females on the beach,
but their very tough,
thick skin saves them
from too much
damage.

Tusk

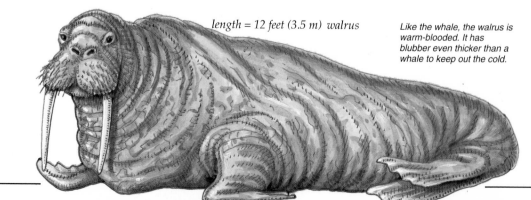

length = 12 feet (3.5 m) walrus

Like the whale, the walrus is
warm-blooded. It has
blubber even thicker than a
whale to keep out the cold.

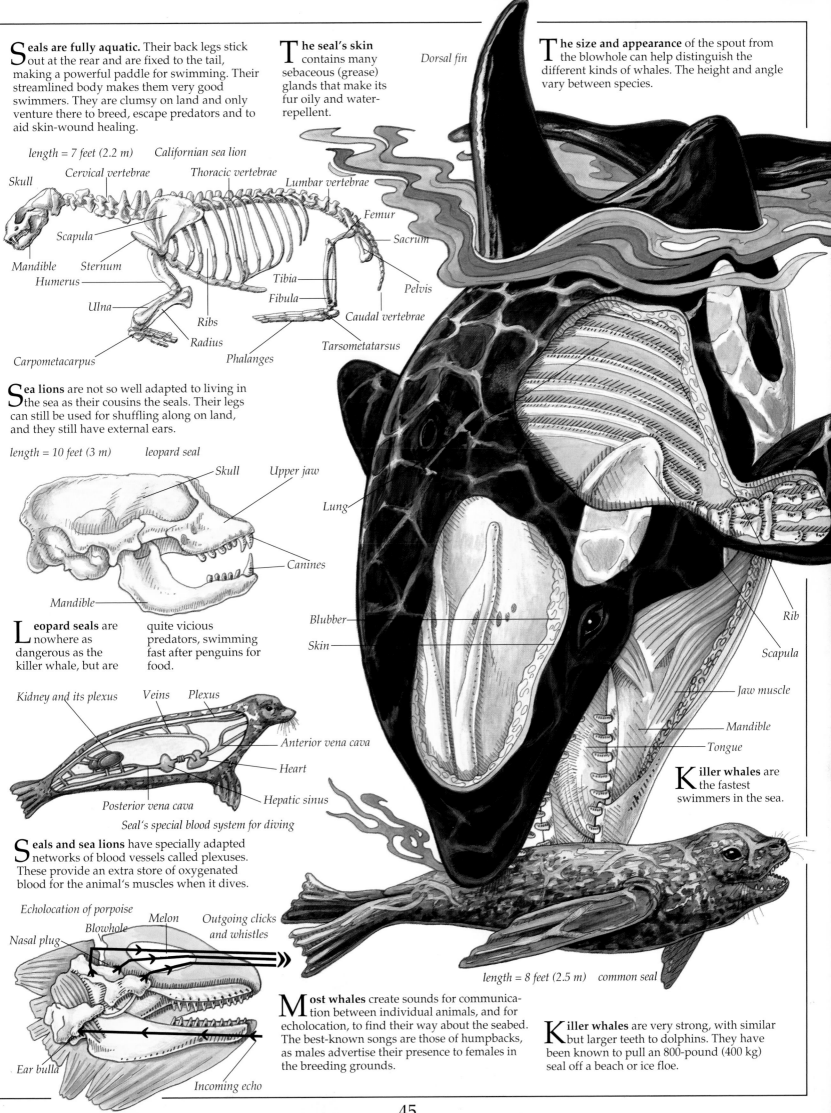

Seals are fully aquatic. Their back legs stick out at the rear and are fixed to the tail, making a powerful paddle for swimming. Their streamlined body makes them very good swimmers. They are clumsy on land and only venture there to breed, escape predators and to aid skin-wound healing.

length = 7 feet (2.2 m) — *Californian sea lion*

Skull
Cervical vertebrae
Thoracic vertebrae
Lumbar vertebrae
Scapula
Femur
Mandible
Sacrum
Sternum
Humerus
Tibia
Pelvis
Ulna
Fibula
Caudal vertebrae
Ribs
Radius
Tarsometatarsus
Carpometacarpus
Phalanges

Sea lions are not so well adapted to living in the sea as their cousins the seals. Their legs can still be used for shuffling along on land, and they still have external ears.

length = 10 feet (3 m) — *leopard seal*

Skull
Upper jaw
Canines
Mandible

Leopard seals are nowhere as dangerous as the killer whale, but are quite vicious predators, swimming fast after penguins for food.

Kidney and its plexus
Veins
Plexus
Anterior vena cava
Heart
Posterior vena cava
Hepatic sinus

Seal's special blood system for diving

Seals and sea lions have specially adapted networks of blood vessels called plexuses. These provide an extra store of oxygenated blood for the animal's muscles when it dives.

Echolocation of porpoise
Blowhole
Melon
Outgoing clicks and whistles
Nasal plug
Ear bulla
Incoming echo

The seal's skin contains many sebaceous (grease) glands that make its fur oily and water-repellent.

The size and appearance of the spout from the blowhole can help distinguish the different kinds of whales. The height and angle vary between species.

Dorsal fin
Lung
Blubber
Skin
Rib
Scapula
Jaw muscle
Mandible
Tongue

Killer whales are the fastest swimmers in the sea.

length = 8 feet (2.5 m) — *common seal*

Most whales create sounds for communication between individual animals, and for echolocation, to find their way about the seabed. The best-known songs are those of humpbacks, as males advertise their presence to females in the breeding grounds.

Killer whales are very strong, with similar but larger teeth to dolphins. They have been known to pull an 800-pound (400 kg) seal off a beach or ice floe.

45

GLOSSARY

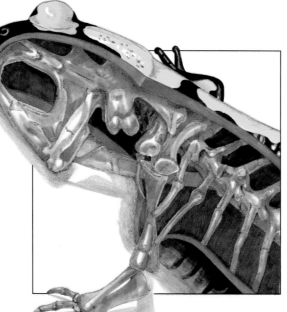

Airfoil An object shaped to produce an upward movement (lift) when it passes through a flow of water or air.

Anterior Situated at, or near, the front end.

Aquatic Living and growing in water.

Bacterium A microscopic, single-celled organism with a simple structure. Plural: Bacteria.

Baleen The bony plates that can be found growing from the palate (roof of the mouth) of certain whales; whalebone.

Binocular vision Able to see objects in three dimensions; stereoscopic vision.

Burrow A hole in the ground that an animal uses for shelter, defense and breeding.

Camouflage Any device or means, especially visual, of disguise, to deceive a predator or prey.

Canine tooth The long, pointed tooth situated between the incisors at the front of an animal's jaw; the eye-tooth.

Carapace The shell that covers the back of some animals, including lobsters, scorpions and tortoises.

Carnassial tooth The cutting tooth of a carnivorous animal; the last premolar tooth of the upper jaw and the first molar tooth in the lower jaw.

Carnivore An animal that eats meat.

Cartilage Skeletal material made from a pearly-white, tough substance; gristle.

Chrysalis Pupa of a butterfly or moth; the third stage of an insect's life, between the larval and adult stages.

Diffusing Spreading out from a single point to cover a wide area.

Digest To convert food, in the stomach, into substances that can be absorbed into the blood or body.

Embryo Animal (or plant) in the early stages of development, before the main organs are complete. The embryo develops within an egg or within the body of the mother.

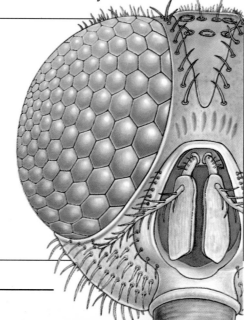

Environment The place and conditions that surround an animal or plant.

Evolution The changes that occur in animals and plants over several generations, which lead to new varieties and species. Evolution is a gradual process, taking place over thousands of years.

Exoskeleton The thick, hard, tough cuticle of an insect, spider or other arthropod; an outer skeleton.

Extinct Describes an animal or plant species that has died out completely; none of the species remains.

Filter A device to strain fine solids from a liquid.

Fluke Lobe of a whale's tail.

Foliage Collection of live plants, twigs and leaves.

Habitat The natural home of an animal or plant.

Herbivore An animal that eats only plants.

Incisor teeth The sharp, chisel-like front teeth of a mammal.

Incubate To sit on eggs before they hatch and to brood young.

Indigenous Describes an animal or plant species that is native to a particular area, i.e., not introduced by humans.

Insulate To keep something apart from contact with cold or electricity.

Invertebrate An animal without a backbone.

Larva First stage of an insect's life cycle when it is different from an adult but able to fend for itself; that which hatches from the egg.

Lateral To do with the side of an animal.

Marine Found in or near the sea.

Migrate To travel from one place to another; commonly used to describe the long journeys to the south made by birds to escape the harsh winters of the northern hemisphere.

Navigate To find one's way when traveling from place to place.

Nocturnal Active at night, rather than in daylight.

Nymph An insect larva that hatches in a well-developed state and which closely resembles the adult. Its wings and reproductive organs are undeveloped. A nymph grows by shedding its skin several times as it reaches adulthood.

Omnivore An animal that eats both plants and other animals.

Operculum A lid that covers the gill slit of a fish or an amphibian. It is also the tough plate in some gastropods that can cover the opening through which the animal withdraws into its shell.

Parasite An organism that lives and feeds in, or on, another animal or plant, doing it harm as it does so.

Pigment Coloring matter found in animal tissue.

Plague A deadly epidemic or disease that sweeps quickly through a whole population.

Polarized A word used to describe waves of light vibrating in one plane.

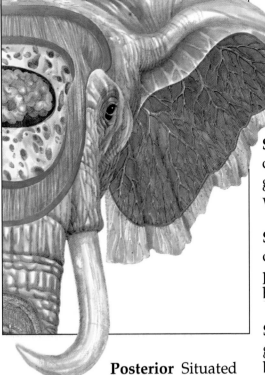

Posterior Situated at, or near, the back or hind end of an animal.

Predator An animal that catches other animals for food.

Prehensile Capable of grasping; often used to describe a tail that has a gripping function.

Prey An animal that is, or may be, eaten by another.

Proboscis A long extension from the nose or mouthparts of some animals; the trunk of an elephant; the elongated mouthparts of some insects.

Radula The rasping tongue of a snail or other gastropod.

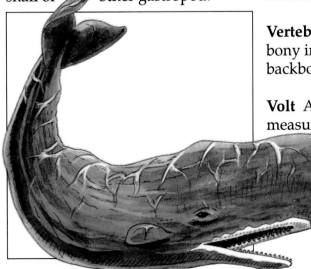

Repellent A substance that repels, repulses, drives away.

Resonator A structure that returns and amplifies sound (makes it louder).

Savanna An area of flat level land covered with low plants such as grass, usually treeless or dotted with trees and small woods.

Scales The thin, flat plates covering fish and reptiles that protect the underlying soft skin and body.

Secretion A substance made by a gland of an animal that is needed by the animal to live or excreted from the body.

Skeleton The bony framework that supports the body of an animal, protects certain organs and provides a means of attachment for muscles and ligaments.

Species A group of similar animals that can breed with one another but which are incapable of breeding with other groups, or species.

Terrestrial Living on land.

Venom The poison produced by some animals and plants as a defense.

Ventral Of the underside of an animal.

Vertebrate An animal that has a bony internal support; the backbone.

Volt An electrical unit that is a measure of the pressure of the electrical current.

Webbed A term used to describe the feet of some animals whose toes are connected by a membrane.

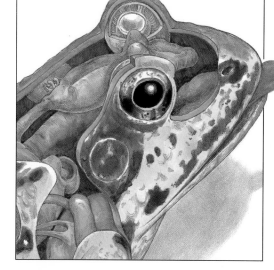

INDEX

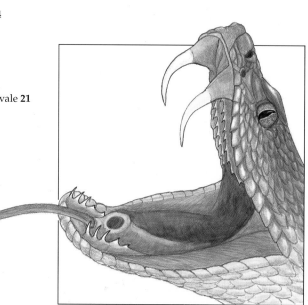